Interpreting Worship

Interpreting Worship

ALAN DUNSTAN
Canon Residentiary and Precentor of Gloucester Cathedral

MOREHOUSE BARLOW
Wilton, Connecticut

First American Edition 1985 by
Morehouse Barlow Co., Inc.
78 Danbury Road
Wilton, Connecticut 06897

ISBN 8192-1357-8

Library of Congress Catalog Card Number 84-62377

Printed in the United States of America

First published in 1984
by A. R. Mowbary & Co., Ltd.
Saint Thomas House, Becket Street
Oxford OX1 1SJ

To my sister

Acknowledgements

The author and publisher wish to express their thanks to the following for permission to reproduce material of which they are the authors, publishers or copyright holders.

Oxford University Press for an extract from *The Renewal of Worship*, ed. Jaspar (quoted by J.G. Huxtable); and for the words of three verses of 'Lord of the boundless curves of space' by Albert F. Bayly (1901-).

Epworth Press for extracts from *Preaching Reassessed* by John Stacey.

Collins Publishers for an extract from *Fame is the Spur* by Howard Spring.

The Royal School of Church Music for an extract from *The Hymn Explosion* by Alan Dunstan.

An extract from *The Alternative Service Book: A Commentary by the Liturgical Commission* (CIO Publishing, 1980) is reproduced by kind permission of the Central Board of Finance of the Church of England.

Cambridge University Press for an extract from *On the Art of Reading* by Sir Arthur Quiller-Couch.

The Society for Promoting Christian Knowledge for extracts from 'Worship and the Pastoral Office' by David Tripp in *The Study of Liturgy*, ed. Jones, Wainwright, Yarnold; *The Paradox of Worship* by Michael Perry; 'Liturgy and her companions' by J.L. Houlden in *The Eucharist Today*, ed. R.C.D. Jasper; 'The Bible and the Liturgy' by Neville Clark in *Getting the Liturgy Right*, ed. R.C.D. Jasper.

An extract from *The Ministry of the Word* by D.W. Cleverley Ford is reprinted by permission of Hodder and Stoughton Limited, © 1979.

The Saint Andrew Press on behalf of The United Reformed Church for a short prayer from *Book of Services*.

Adam and Charles Black Publishers for an extract from *The Shape of the Liturgy* by Dom Gregory Dix (Dacre Press).

BBC Publications and Archbishop Michael Ramsey for an extract from the Foreword to *New Every Morning*.

Marshall, Morgan & Scott Publications Ltd for extracts from *Renewal in Worship* by Michael Marshall.

SCM Press Ltd for extracts from *Christian Faith and Life* by William Temple, *Worship and Mission* by J.G. Davies, and *The Shaking of the Foundations* by Paul Tillich.

Hinshaw Music Inc. for the text paraphrase of 'There in God's Garden' by Erik Routley, copyright © 1976 by Hinshaw Music Inc.

Contents

Preface

This book is based upon a course of eight lectures given at the annual Bible school of St Giles-in-the-Fields, Holborn, in the autumn of 1982. The weekly attendance at the lectures was between 100 and 200 and included ordained and lay members from various branches of the Christian Church; some were involved in particular forms of ministry, and others regard the school as a means of adult Christian education. The aim of the lectures was to examine some biblical concepts of God and to enquire how they might be expressed practically in Christian worship. I am grateful to the Rector, the Reverend G. C. Taylor, for his invitation to deliver the lectures, to the Registrar, my friend the Reverend Iain MacKenzie, for his kindness and hospitality, and to those present for their warm reception. The lectures have had to be somewhat revised for publication, and I am very grateful to another old friend, Miss Freda Grainger, for typing the script for the publishers.

A.D.

Foreword

It is a privilege to be asked to write a Foreword to Canon Dunstan's book, if only because I count myself among the very many who acknowledge his authority in liturgical affairs. Anyone who might be inclined to question that authority need only visit Gloucester Cathedral, where Alan Dunstan's sure touch as Precentor has improved the standard of our offering of worship quite dramatically since he joined us in 1978. I pay this small tribute gladly and willingly, even though the only reference to Bishops I can find in the following pages might suggest that the species is universally absent-minded!

I hope readers will note the style – direct, balanced, vigorous. You cannot fail to detect the rhythms of the preacher who rarely fails to hold his audience. But you cannot fail either to sense the ordered and disciplined progressions of thought which mark the natural and experienced teacher. The book is a delight to read.

Above all, Canon Dunstan decisively and persuasively relates worship and doctrine, insisting at every point that what we do (and often fail to do) in church services is directly connected to our beliefs about and in God. And he does this without, in any chapter, losing touch with the straightforward practicalities of the matter – the choice of hymns, or the dangers lurking in 'horizontal prayers', for example.

So we have, in manageable form, a useful tool for anyone who is called to lead Christian worship, whether they be the Church of England vicar in the post – ASB era, the Free Church minister, or the layperson called from time to time to perform such a ministry. We also have a study-book for the Church Council which cares about its weekly offering of worship, or the discussion group seeking to grow in the truth of things. I hope it will be widely read.

†John Gloucestr:

1. THE GOD WHOM WE WORSHIP

Why worship?

Most people who go to church are called upon to justify the peculiarity. Worship with the Christian community does not seem a necessity to many who profess belief in God and reverence for Jesus Christ. When the exercise has been attempted, it has often seemed boring, unreal and even hypocritical. There are umpteen reasons for staying away from the local church.

In this book we are concerned with some biblical insights of God and their bearing upon worship. But the Bible simply does not tackle the question 'Why worship?', much less give an answer to it. Many chapters in the early books of the Bible deal with the way in which worship should be offered – with the sanctuary and the lampstand, the vesture of the priest and the nature of sacrifice. The Bible also resorts to admonition to observe the details of worship. Old Testament writers often declare that evil and disaster come because of the neglect of the Sabbath or misuse of it.

The New Testament is tantalizingly reticent about worship. Of course the communities from which it sprang and for which it was written had experienced Baptism and celebrated the Eucharist. We have fragments, indeed, of prayers and hymns and blessings; but the New Testament writers always assumed that their readers would know where all these things belonged, and could hardly have foreseen that two thousand years later we should be trying to put the jigsaw puzzle together. The New Testament does not even contain much by way of admonition, except in the letter to the Hebrews which seems, among other things, designed to recall believers to their early enthusiasm. They are told:

> We ought to see how each of us may best arouse others to love and active goodness, not staying away from our meetings, as some do, but rather encouraging one another, all the more because you see the Day drawing near. (Heb.10.24,25)

In all this we see that the Bible, despite all its variety of date and setting, never argues the case for worship. It always assumes worship. It assumes worship because of the God it portrays. Therefore 'Why worship?' is secondary to the question 'Why God?'. What we believe about God must be the starting point for the discussion of worship in this book – just as it is the starting point for most questions about the Christian faith, and, indeed, wider questions about life itself. The question 'What do you believe about God?' is more important than 'Why do you believe in God?' because the word 'God' can mean all sorts of different things – even within Christian circles themselves. J. B. Phillips, who did so much to make the New Testament intelligible to people of the fifties once wrote a book with the title *Your God is Too Small*. In the first part of it, he drew out some of the associations which the word 'God' had in people's minds. Thus the chapter headings had such intriguing titles as 'Resident Policeman', 'Parental Hangover', 'Grand Old Man', 'Meek and Mild', Heavenly Bosom', 'Managing Director', 'Perennial Grievance', 'Pale Galilean' and finally, 'Assorted'. [1]

These are travesties of the truth about God – or, at best, one-sided conceptions of his nature. In these chapters, we shall be thinking of some biblical concepts of God – bearing in mind that the disclosure of his nature and activity is the main concern of all those assorted writings that we call the Bible. The next chapter will be concerned with the holiness of God, that he is above us as well as with us, beyond us as well as amongst us, and that, for the biblical writers he is more than the sum total of human aspirations and human experience. We shall go on to think of the diversity that is in God; for although the books of the Bible emanate basically from the same race, they yet provide manifold ideas of God, coupled with affirmations about his consistency that are expressed in phrases like 'steadfast love'. We shall see how appreciation of his manifold nature can protect us from thinking of him just as 'perennial grievance' or 'heavenly bosom'. The remaining five chapters will explore his relationship with men and women. Once again, the biblical writers say next to nothing about God-in-himself; they are always concerned with God in relationship to the world he has made, and to men and women made in his image. He is a God who speaks to us. 'Thus saith the Lord' or 'This is the very word of the Lord' is the repeated claim of the prophets; and in the fourth gospel, God's manifestation in Jesus is called 'the Word'. He is a God who listens — one who hears and receives the prayers and desires and aspirations of his people. He is a God who meets his people, who promises to be with individuals and among the chosen community. 'I am with you till the end of time' is the promise at the close of St Matthew's gospel — the gift of the Holy Spirit that of St John. The relationship is not one-sided; for God receives the praise of his people, their offerings of mind and body and heart, and he uses this offering of themselves and their gifts to fulfil his purposes in the world. So finally, he is a God who sends his people out as agents and instruments of his loving will.

These concepts hardly exhaust the nature of God, but they help to answer the question, 'Why worship?'. They show us why the Bible does not address itself to the question. For if God in any way corresponds to what we have been saying about him, there must be worship. If in all his holiness, he is concerned with us, wants to give us things, asks things of us, there must be contact. What is

3

true in general must be true in particular. A lady once said that she had no need to pray because she was praying all the time. Most of us are more honest and more modest. We realize that we shall never begin to approach the state of 'always praying' unless we sometimes pray. This is true of all forms of worship.

Perhaps we need not spend too long in arguing why this worship cannot simply be individual, but involves us in relationship with other people. Quite simply, this is the way that we are made, and every day brings fresh evidence of the fact that we cannot live unto ourselves, but are connected one with another. To take the most drastic example of this, it is evident that the use of nuclear weapons in any one part of the world would have fearful consequences for every part of the world. John Wesley's dictum 'the Bible knows nothing of solitary religion' may be an exaggeration, but it recognizes that the nature of God and the nature of man mean that there must be a Christian society. Jesus did not train his disciples in a series of private interviews; he trained them together.

What is worship?

The concepts of God that we have been considering help us to establish some characteristics of worship, to have some idea of what are its contents. It will include adoration and reverence for the one who is both identified with us and apart from us. If he is a God who speaks to us, it will require attention to the manner in which he has chosen to speak, and will involve reading and exposition of the Scriptures. A listening God makes the whole range of what we call prayer a part of worship. His meeting with us in special ways involves the sacramental and symbolic. Since he receives the gifts of men and women, worship must involve that which we have to offer.

So what is worship? It is essentially our response to

what God has revealed of himself. Through it we recognize the nature and claims of God upon us. A few years ago, it was fashionable to talk of 'worship feelings' and 'worship experiences', and students were encouraged to take note of the emotion of a football match, or the atmosphere engendered when a few friends sat down to listen to music. Here are pointers to what might be the fruits of Christian worship, but that worship depends basically on the Christian revelation. It is concerned with the saving acts of God in the past in order that his saving nature and activity may be realized now. It unites his people in love and service to him.

If this is true, it is hardly necessary to argue the priority of worship. As William Temple once wrote:

> People are always thinking that conduct is supremely important, and that because prayer helps it, therefore prayer is good. That is true as far as it goes: still truer is it to say that worship is of supreme importance and conduct tests it. [2]

And a writer of our own times, David Tripp, describes worship as that which

> manifests the spiritual significance of the world in which the laity work out their vocations. [3]

The realities of worship

Such quotations are splendid. But the truth is that the worship many people experience does not correspond to the worship thus described. The actualities of worship seem far removed from the high-falutin things that are said about it. In how many local churches does worship 'manifest the spiritual significance of the world' in which we have 'to work out our own vocations.'? When people ask the question, 'Why worship?', they are probably not thinking so much in general terms as of particular places like Barchester Cathedral, St Silas' Church or Zion Chapel. The worship of such places seems somewhat distant from the worship we have been trying to describe. Perhaps we should not be surprised at how few people go to church, but rather be surprised at how many do so.

But worshippers must honestly recognize that some of the fault may lie with themselves. It may be that they have thought too much of what they might get and too little of what they might give; it may be that they have taken very little trouble to understand the worship in which they are engaged. Christian people can still be, moreover, unhappily dismissive of ways of worship that are not their own. A generation ago, it was common in Protestant circles to speak of Roman or Anglo-Catholic worship as 'a lot of bowing and scraping'. Bowing there certainly was – in plenty; but who ever managed to identify *scraping*? Anglicans sometimes refer to their own special services and those of the Free Churches as 'hymn-sandwiches'. It is intended to be pejorative – but what is wrong with a sandwich if it is decently and imaginatively made? And we are beginning to realize that Christian worship cannot be immediately and entirely intelligible to anyone who drops in on it. Of course every effort must be made to welcome the casual visitor, and of course the atmosphere of worship or the friendship of the congregation can speak for themselves. But worship itself has to be learned.

That does not quite let our churches off the hook. So let us consider three criticisms of worship as it is often conceived or devised.

First, worship is like a boat that has gathered many barnacles about its keel. The difficulty lies in determining what is barnacle and what is boat. One example of this belongs to the period in which revision of the Anglican liturgy was in progress. There was some discussion as to where 'the prayer of humble access' should be 'put', and

6

groups in parishes were sometimes invited to discuss the question. The assumption among many people was that this prayer was essential to the Communion Service. But is it? It was compiled by Cranmer from various sources and inserted into the Mass in order to help people prepare themselves for communion. In the second Prayer Book (1552) it was built into the structure of the service, and theological as well as devotional reasons began to be cited for its position. The beautiful prayer has meant much to countless thousands of worshippers. But it is a piece of embroidery, not part of the fabric of the service. It is not to be supposed that all adornments and enrichments are like barnacles that ought to be scraped away. But this is merely an example of how the secondary can come to be seen as primary. Even the very trivial can seem important. In Compton Mackenzie's novel about a Cornish parish, the vicar, who has already annoyed his parishioners over ritual, adds fuel to the fire by appointing as churchwarden not one of the farmers, but a very humble labourer. But the poor man is conscious of the inadequacies of his wardrobe for such an elevated status, and despite all the vicar's reassurances, says, 'Whoever heard of a churchwarden without a black coat?'.[4]

Secondly, worship has a tendency to get rigid and stultified. This may seem an extraordinary statement in view of the liturgical revolution that has been going on in all the Churches over the last twenty years. It is true that we have given much attention to language and structure. But we have given far less to the presentation and 'staging' of worship. *Getting the Liturgy Right*, by members of the Joint Liturgical Group, is an essay in this direction. But worship seems so often planned without reference to the actual congregation taking part in it or the building in which it is being held. Michael Marshall presents an illustration of such:

From the outset everything about the worship is

borrowed and imported secondhand from a faded and jaded form of worship. . . . It is just trying to be what it is not. . . . There are two and a half servers, and one of them is struggling to carry a cross at the head of what is parading as a procession . . . (which) enters the church as if it were the vast nave of a European cathedral. The sermon is preached from the pulpit in a style which would be more appropriate to Hyde Park Corner. The collection during the hymn is a major operation engaging the only two men from the congregation in carrying large dusty wooden plates in which a rather obviously small collection is pompously and pretentiously collected and blessed. A bread board bearing a loaf of bread and breadsaw, together with a bottle of sanctuary wine is rather uneasily, though self-consciously, carried down the central aisle in what is intended to be an offertory procession, though in practice the aisle is only twenty five feet long between the back member of the congregation and the priest.

And the Bishop goes on

Everything will require retailoring if this small act of worship is to ring true and lift those present into the one great act of worship in heaven. [5]

It is just this retailoring that is so necessary in many places. Search must be made for what is appropriate to the people and their building. At an evening Communion service in what was once a celebrated Free Church, four large chalices stood on the communion table, but the congregation numbered seventeen. Such a service conducted as though seven hundred were present is not only unreal but disheartening to the seventeen.

The third criticism is akin to the first two, but goes

deeper. In the course of a much quoted essay entitled 'Liturgy and her Companions', J. L. Houlden wrote:

> The present-day Christian will surely wish, as he approaches the task of thinking about his worship, to use the insights of anthropology, psychology and sociology which bear upon it – not in order to secularize or de-Christianize his work, but in order to undertake it with his mind alert to everything that concerns it.
>
> It is no exaggeration to say that modern liturgy-making has scarcely glanced into any of these teritories. 'Liturgical principles' have hardly begun to rub against 'biblical principles' or 'doctrinal principles' let alone considerations arising from more basic fields of study.[6]

This judgement, made originally about the Series 3 Communion Service, may be a little harsh. Liturgy is involved with continuity, and there have been periods of history where the very stability of the liturgy has protected the Church from too easy an acceptance of every theological and cultural fashion. And it can be claimed that some contemporary prayers and hymns come nearer to what Mr Houlden suggests than the more staple diet of worship. But we cannot ignore the danger that liturgy will grow remote from everyday experience, that its bells will ring even more faintly for potential worshippers, and, most serious of all, that it will be regarded and used simply as a form of escapism.

The task in worship

All these considerations show us how much there is to be done by framers of liturgy and leaders of worship. Much thought has been given to its shape and its language; it is likely that the shape of our new services will be with us for some years to come, though we shall seek improvements in language if it is to be powerful and memorable, as well as clear and intelligible. But there are other things to which we must give energy and imagination. There is the whole question of its setting; the search for what is appropriate to particular places and to particular congregations. There is the continued need to secure the best standards, within the means and abilities of a particular community, of reading, music and movement. There is need for discriminating choice in all the variety of material now available for worship; it is like a garden in which there is continual need of pruning and hoeing. There is still room for newly created material (particularly in prayers, songs and special services) which will reflect the actualities of the life we live and the society to which we belong. Worship needs a rhythm and continuity, together with that which always freshens and enlivens it. All this reveals the importance of taking time and trouble over the details of worship. This does not mean fuss; but it is, perhaps, the modern application of those interminable and apparently tedious chapters of the Old Testament which deal so lengthily with the sanctuary and its furnishings.

However, there are other pages of the Old Testament where prophets warn us that care for the details of worship is not enough. The true worship of God is not in the end secured by carefully devised and beautifully executed services. What matters more is the attitude of the worshippers. But that still means that our liturgical gatherings shall reveal the nature and claims of the God whom we worship.

Notes
1. J. B. Phillips, *Your God is too Small*, Epworth Press, 1952.
2. William Temple, *Christian Faith and Life*, SCM Press, 1931, p.19.

3. David Tripp, 'Worship and the Pastoral Office' in *Study of Liturgy* (ed. Jones, Wainwright, Yarnold) SPCK, 1978, p. 512.
4. Compton Mackenzie, *The Heavenly Ladder*.
5. Michael Marshall, *Renewal in Worship*, Marshall, Morgan & Scott, 1982, pp. 67–68.
6. J. L. Houlden, 'Liturgy and her Companions' in *The Eucharist Today* (ed. R. C. D. Jasper) SPCK, 1974, p. 171.

2. THE GOD WHO IS HOLY

We often hear the complaint that contemporary worship has lost all sense of mystery. In this chapter, we shall first investigate what is meant by this charge. Secondly, we shall ask what is the nature of the mystery that should be enshrined in worship – in other words, what we understand by the holiness of God. Thirdly, we shall try to see how such insights of God's holiness can be applied to the actual practice of worship.

The 'lost mystery'

What exactly has been lost?

Thirty years ago, the Roman Catholic Mass was in Latin. The people had translations and books of devotion which they were encouraged to use in the course of it, but they were not expected to follow the service in detail. Indeed parts of the eucharistic prayer were said secretly and inaudibly, and the priest normally had his back to the congregation. Reception of Holy Communion was occasional. Almost at the stroke of a pen, all this disappeared – though there had been a period of experimentation. The whole of the Mass appeared in the vernacular; the people were encouraged to follow not only its action, but its wording. The priest faced the people, and laity began to read lessons and lead intercessions. General communion became the norm. In some places, the music which had accompanied the Latin texts tended to become redundant. Hymns written by Protestants were discovered and used. At a point in the eucharistic prayer, the priest said 'Let us proclaim the mystery of faith', but some felt that it was precisely the *mystery* of faith that had disappeared.

Liturgical revision has been much more drastic for Roman Catholics than for Christians of other Churches. For most of the present century, strict observance of the Prayer Book has been rare. Alterations permitted by the abortive revision of 1928 have been commonly used, and there were churches where the form of the Communion service bore little resemblance to that of 1662. After 1965, Series 2 and Series 3 were stages along the road to The Alternative Service Book 1980. The title of the latter was chosen advisedly, and the date stamped on the cover suggests that it is not designed for perpetuity. This is in contrast to the American Episcopal Church where traditional and modern services exist side by side in a new edition of the Book of Common Prayer. Nevertheless, fears have been constantly expressed that both the Prayer Book and the Authorized Version of the Bible will find themselves phased out of regular Anglican worship.

The Free Churches have, of course, a tradition of greater elasticity in worship. Nevertheless an attempt to create a hymn book that would be common to the United Reformed and the Methodist Churches failed partly because of the insistence of the Methodist Conference that the book must contain a fixed proportion of Charles Wesley's hymns. Overtly, this was not so much a matter of 'mystery' as of doctrine. But the place of the hymn book in Methodist affections has been comparable to that of the Prayer Book in the Church of England.

It is not easy to be specific about 'the lost mystery'. It is inevitably subjective; it is something felt rather than something that can be clearly demonstrated. In the Church of England, it is certainly connected with language − which had for so long been largely that of the sixteenth and seventeenth centuries. The mumblings and grumblings have been articulated in a book called *No*

Alternative[1]. This is largely an indictment of The Alternative Service Book 1980, and, with varying degrees of fervour, a defence of the Book of Common Prayer. Contributions to the book range from the near-hysterical and the journalistically clever to essays that are scholarly and thoughtful. Amongst the latter we find Canon Vanstone's insistence that people need 'space' as well as 'place' in which to worship, and the assertion made in different ways by David Cockerell, I. R. Thompson and Chris O'Neill that language should somehow point beyond itself, and have a 'quality of transparency'.

It is not difficult to assemble from modern liturgies and modern translations of the Bible a host of examples to prove the case that they are flat and insipid. But the preface to The Alternative Service Book 1980 says of the words of that book:

> Those who use them do well to recognize their transience and imperfection; to treat them as a ladder, not a goal.

And the fact that the book has not been enacted for all time is a challenge to do something better. But it can also be claimed that parts of the new liturgy have begun to acquire an evocative power of their own; the second proper preface for 'the Cross' and the post-communion prayers in Rite A can be cited as examples of these.

But the complaint about 'lost mystery' is not confined to language. It is connected with the multiplicity of books and the difficulty of finding places; with the increased role of the laity and the diminution of much traditional ritual; with the placing of the altar in the midst of the congregation rather than at some distance from them; but perhaps most of all because in many modern liturgical uses, worshippers come into visual and physical contact with one another. It is alleged that the cumulative effect of all these things is a replacement of the transcendent by the immanent, and that the majesty and 'otherness' of God seem to be edged out. It is to the nature of God's holiness that we must therefore turn.

Which mystery?

The second part of this chapter is governed by a text – Hosea 11:9 'I am God and not man, the Holy One in your midst'. This text suggests at one and the same time the 'other-ness' of God *and* his nearness to his people, his majesty and incomparability with any created thing *and* his involvement with men and women. We must think of these two characteristics together, because they belong together. Holiness is a way of describing the uniqueness and perfection of God. But it is impossible to separate the *nature* of God from the *activity* of God. The biblical tradition, as we have seen, knows next to nothing of God in himself: its constant theme is God's relationship with his world. The God who appears to Moses in the burning bush is the God who has 'seen the affliction' of his people. 'The holy God shows himself holy in righteousness' says the first Isaiah. The holiness and apart-ness of God are manifested in his undeviating purpose of righteousness and love which find their supreme expression in his offering of Christ to the world, and in Christ's self-offering to the Father. There is an apart-ness about all this, because human dedication and human love for all their grandeur are fickle and transient by contrast with the holy God.

It is the apprehension of this holiness that inspires awe and even a kind of dread among people. For Moses at the burning bush the place becomes 'holy ground'. Isaiah becomes aware that he is lost when he has his great vision of Yahweh in his temple. Peter jumps back into the sea when he sees the risen Christ standing on the shore. Paul is blinded by what happens on the Damascus road. Although the writer of the letter to the Hebrews is for ever contrasting the new revelation with the old, he still believes that 'our God is a consuming fire' and is to be worshipped 'with reverence and awe'.

One of the seminal books of our own century has been Rudolf Otto's *The Idea of the Holy*. [2] Perhaps this book was as responsible as any for bringing the word 'numinous' into common currency, and it is significant that the book was an enquiry into the non-rational aspects of religion. And one of the criticisms of modern liturgy is that it is all too rational.

'Worship and Mystery' is a chapter heading in two books published during the last decade. Michael Perry in *The Paradox of Worship* [3] asks early in his chapter the question 'How do we bring the feeling of the numinous into our worship?' and corrects himself in his answer:

> As soon as we frame that question, we realize the sheer impertinence of asking it. The feeling of the numinous is the human side of a divine revelation, and it is not for us to expect to manipulate it to order, or to manipulate it within the confines of liturgical engineering. The numinous blows where it lists, and we cannot dare to command it.

When Wordsworth wrote his famous lines [4] above Tintern Abbey:

> I have felt
> A presence that disturbs me with the joy
> Of elevated thoughts; a sense sublime
> Of something far more deeply interfused
> Whose dwelling is the light of setting suns,
> And the round ocean, and the living air,
> And the blue sky, and in the mind of man,

we are not to suppose that he journeyed to the Wye Valley in order to get an experience like that. It happened. Leslie

Weatherhead, for so many years the much loved and much listened-to minister of the City Temple says:

> Vauxhall Station on a murky November evening is not a setting one would claim for a revelation of God. [5]

Yet he tells us that it was on a journey from that station that, as a young student, he came to some perception of what God wanted him to do and to be. An anthology of religious experience by Michael Peppard is significantly entitled *The Unattended Moment*. [6] Such moments are. They are not to be sought and they cannot be conjured up. John Wesley spoke of certain religious feelings as 'sweet-meats' to be enjoyed now and again, but not the staple diet of Christians.

The Dean of Worcester also has a chapter on 'Worship and Mystery' in his book *Questioning Worship*. [7] Here he emphasizes what we have already noted in this brief biblical sketch – namely that it was the vocation of the prophets to 'de-sacralize' the holiness of God, and to interpret it in terms of moral purity and loving-kindness. This brings us again to our central theme – the nature of the mystery which we are celebrating. It has been succinctly expressed by Father Michael Richards:

> There are liturgies that we have made mysterious by turning them into linguistic monuments. Before we put our worship into words and music, ritual and vestment, we must be sure that we know and begin to understand the true nature of the mystery we celebrate. Christianity took the term 'mystery' and developed its meaning, making it stand now not for secrecy, obscurity and concealment, but for declaration and making plain. [8]

This is the sense in which the word is used in the letter to the Ephesians. In the first chapter, mystery is seen as manifestation – in the coming of Jesus Christ among us, in his life and ministry, in his cross and resurrection, in his ascension and the promise that all things will be consummated in him. This mystery is apprehended through the Holy Spirit who makes Christ our contemporary, who makes word and sacrament real to our hearts and minds, who leads us into that truth that God has in store for us.

The holiness of God is made known to us through his saving acts, and in the saving acts of Christ lies the true Christian mystery. Writing of the language of the new services, David Frost has said:

> Those who have incarnation, crucifixion and resurrection to proclaim need no humanly created veils in which to shroud their mysteries. [9]

Of course the saving acts of Christ have to be expressed in words, in symbols, in ritual. What matters supremely in worship is that the words, symbols and ritual do point to the saving acts, and not away from them. So we end this section and this catena of quotations with one more – from an almost forgotten bishop in the first half of this century. Writing of the Eucharist, on which he held strong and controversial views, J. W. Hunkin said:

> Always room must be left in the service for the sense of Great Mystery – not some petty mystery next door to magic, but the Great Mystery of life and death, of Redemption and the love of God. [10]

Apprehending the mystery

How can these insights about holiness and mystery be applied practically to the planning and leadership of worship? Before answering that question, we must heed again the warning that has already been sounded. The *feeling* of awe and reverence cannot be induced by the most carefully planned worship. As Michael Perry said, the question, 'How do we bring the feeling of the numinous into our worship?' is both impertinent and improper. It happens or it doesn't. Back in 1923, Rudolf Otto maintained that the old jumbled Lutheran rite gave more opportunity for the numinous than what he called 'carefully arranged schemes worked out with the balance of an essay with nothing unaccountable, nothing accidental'.[11] This sounds a bit like the arguments with which we began – arguments for the Latin Mass or the 1662 Prayer Book on the grounds that there is more mystery about them. But in Christian worship we are not thinking of any old mystery, but of the Christian mystery. And the holiness which we seek to acknowledge and reverence must be the holiness of God as revealed in the Scriptures.

This means in the first place that Christian worship must be centred around the Christian mystery, and that its basic content is the rehearsal of the saving acts of God, with our response in praise, thanksgiving, penitence, intercession and dedication. The saving acts are rehearsed in the readings from the Scriptures and the celebration of the sacraments. Most of the mainstream Churches have so remodelled their eucharistic prayers so that the central tenets of the Christian faith are specifically mentioned in them. Whereas the 'consecration prayer' of 1662 seemed exclusively concerned with the cross, the eucharistic prayers of the ASB refer to the whole activity of God in creation, redemption and sanctification, and parallels to this may be found in the prayers of other Churches. This is a vast improvement, but it does not mean that the Christian creed has to be carefully spelt out in every act of worship. Such an idea leads us back to the notion that worship is not valid unless a certain form of words is used. Anglicans above all ought to know that the mere recital of creeds is no guarantee of orthodoxy! There is, moreover, room for the allusive and the subtle in worship. You do not, for example, have to be constantly *mentioning* the Holy Spirit in order to be referring to him.

But having said this, we must also be sure that certain elements of the Christian mystery do not get distorted in our worship. There are Christmas services in plenty which pay very clouded witness to the doctrine of the incarnation. The festival of Nine Lessons and Carols, regarded in many Christian communities as *de rigueur* has not been an unmixed blessing for the Christian Church. Some Easter services suggest that Good Friday has been cancelled out, and Ascensiontide can suggest no more than the happy ending of a story.

Beginning worship

But people have to be helped to respond to this content. This means, among other things, that attention must be given to the immediate preparation of worshippers for worship. It is a more unfamiliar exercise than it was in days when churches were at the heart of communities, or when chapels dominated the Welsh valleys. Most of us need to go through the process that Quakers call 'centring down'. When you go into many churches for worship, it is like entering an Eastern market. Some people want to defend this hubbub. David Austerberry in *Celebrating the Liturgy*[12] thinks it is wholly natural that members of God's family should greet one another and exchange news, and he advocates that the notices should be given out at this point – though he does recommend a period of corporate silence when all this has been done. But most of us need rather more.

Last minute fussiness is to be avoided like the plague. There should be a point, long before the service is due to begin, by which hymn boards are put up, candles lit, and servers, choristers and other officials stop their perambulations. If this is done, stillness can be achieved in the church building, and an atmosphere of recollection encouraged. The presence of small children can make this more difficult, but it is important that each congregation should achieve as much stillness as is possible. And what is desirable for those in the body of the church is equally so for those in the vestry.

A congregation can be further helped towards this in at least three ways that are by no means mutually exclusive. There can be something to look at – not necessarily a cross, not necessarily a picture, though often one of them – but perhaps a device that is appropriate to the time of the year, or even a flower arrangement; something that expresses the nature of the mystery which we are to celebrate. Then there can be something to listen to – a carefully chosen piece of music would not necessarily have to be played on an organ, for the use of other instruments can help other people to make their contribution to worship. We tend to treat instrumentalists rather shabbily – often allowing the voluntary, which may be the result of long training and much practice simply to be background music for our own conversation. Thirdly, there can be something to think about – a verse or a short meditation printed for that purpose on the notices sheet. In the Church of Scotland, the Bible is usually brought into the church shortly before the service is due to begin; in one church outside the Presbyterian tradition, this happened five minutes before the service, and the notices sheet indicated that this was the cue for stillness and the immediate preparation for worship.

We all need to feel at home in our Father's house and yet never to forget that it is *his* house. This is another way of expressing the truth that the Holy One is in our midst. The ordering of worship as well as the words spoken must point to this truth. Thus, there must be times of silence as well as of speech; times of solemnity as well as of informality; and room for spontaneity within order. And no

21

act of worship should leave us totally unchallenged. At a Pentecost service, one woman stood rigid and disapproving as the 'Peace' was exchanged, but a moment later was singing very lustily 'Come down, O love divine'. What did she think 'love divine' really was? The prophets would tell us that the first test of our worship is our attitude to those around us.

Details of worship must not become an obsession; for the people of God are not all clergy or servers. But constantly renewed vigilance, sensitivity and imagination are required of all who play some part in leading worship, and expectancy of mind as well as enthusiasm of heart must be found in the worshipping community itself. Our styles of worship are largely man-made; and they can be remade by men and women who are seeking and affirming the Holy One in their midst.

Notes

1. *No Alternative*, ed. David Martin and Peter Mullen, Blackwells, 1981.
2. Rudolf Otto, *The Idea of the Holy*, OUP, 1923, 1950.
3. Michael Perry, *The Paradox of Worship*, SPCK, 1977.
4. Perry, op. cit., p.85.
5. Leslie Weatherhead, *The Christian Agnostic*, Hodder & Stoughton, 1965, p.39.
6. Michael Peppard, *The Unattended Moment*, SCM, 1976.
7. T. G. A. Baker, *Questioning Worship*, SCM, 1976.
8. Perry, op. cit., p.93.
9. D. L. Frost, *The Eucharist Today*, ed. Jasper, SPCK, 1974, p.145.
10. J. W. Hunkin, *The Gospel for Tomorrow*, Penguin, 1941, p.75.
11. Otto, op. cit., p.214.
12. David Austerberry, *Celebrating the Liturgy*, Mowbray, 1980.

3. THE GOD WHO IS MANIFOLD

'When in former times God spoke to our forefathers, he spoke in fragmentary and varied fashion through the prophets. . . . ' So begins the letter to the Hebrews in the translation of the New English Bible. We shall in this chapter be concerned with the very diverse view of God presented in the Scriptures; we shall see how lectionaries seek to witness to that diversity; and finally we shall ask how the Scriptures can be most effectively used and presented in worship.

Many images of God

In 1920 *On the Art of Reading* was published. This was a celebrated course of lectures given in Cambridge by Sir Arthur Quiller-Couch ('Q'). Two of the lectures were 'On Reading the Bible' and in one of them is a very telling illustration of how the Bible was put together and presented in the Authorized Version. 'Q' asked his hearers to imagine a variety of books – among them *Paradise Lost*, Darwin's *Descent of Man*, the *Anglo-Saxon Chronicle*, *Domesday Book*, Palgrave's *Golden Treasury*, Newman's *Apologia*, Donne's *Sermons*, Swinburne's *Poems and Ballads*. He asked people to imagine further all these books bound together in one great volume. Many of the authors' names are lost and some have found their way to the wrong places so that Charles II is credited with *The Anatomy of Melancholy*! Some of the titles are not those of the author, but invented by a committee. All the poetry is printed as prose, and all the prose is broken up into short verses. 'Have we done?' asks 'Q' – 'By no means; having effected all this, let us pepper the result over with italics and numerals, print it in double columns with a marginal gutter on either side, each gutter pouring down an inky flow of references and cross-references . . . it remains only then to appoint it to be read in churches'.[1]

Perhaps it was 'Q's strictures which helped the publication of an attractive volume called *The Bible Designed to be Read as Literature* which, although it followed in the main the text of the Authorized Version, tried to divide the contents according to style and subject matter and certainly to present poetry as poetry. Modern translations of the Bible usually make a distinction between prose and poetry, insert inverted commas, and provide helpful subheadings. The *appearance* of such Bibles is undeniably an improvement on the traditional King James Version, whatever one may think of the quality of the English that is used.

And it is now universally accepted that we have an enormous variety of material within the covers of the Bible. Consequently, there is also variety in the ways in which God is presented to us. He is seen as father, law-giver, judge, warrior, shepherd, husband, mother – as well as in the more theological categories of creator, redeemer, sanctifier. The same variety is sometimes found within individual books, though such books, as we know, may themselves be composite in authorship. Thus in the prophet, Hosea, God appears first as a wronged husband, later as father/mother, and in between as judge. Similarly the Psalms – again composite in authorship and date – seem to oscillate between a God of relentless severity and a God of infinite tenderness. Some of us would want to give much weight to the fact that all these concepts come to us through human eyes and human voices, and that they therefore reflect the particular circumstances and situations in which they were first spoken or written.

During the present century the theological pendulum has swung between emphasis on the *unity* and *variety* of the Bible. An instance of this may be seen in the relation-ship of prophet to priest in the Old Testament. Some scholars have seen the great prophets as totally opposed to the system of priesthood and sacrifice because its corrup-tions have made it irredeemable. More recently, perhaps, the prophets have been seen within the cultic process denouncing its misuse rather than its practice. This radi-cal over-simplification of an intricate point of Old Testament scholarship simply illustrates the point.

We began with a text which we did not complete. 'When in former times God spoke to our forefathers, he spoke in fragmentary and varied fashion' begins the letter to the Hebrews, but it goes on, 'but in this final age he has spoken to us in the Son'. He is described in St John as 'the Word' and has often been conceived as the one who sums up all words. Could we not say that all the fragmentary and varied ideas of God are therefore made coherent in the New Testament? This is not quite so simple as it sounds, because in the New Testament itself we have various por-trayals of Jesus. One illustration of this may be found in the passion narratives, and in the 'words' on the cross which each of the evangelists ascribes to Jesus. Again, there was a theological fashion in the nineteenth century that sought to put Paul versus Jesus, and this has not quite disappeared from popular thought. Following Luther's celebrated dismissal of James as 'a right strawy epistle', James and Paul have often been set against each other.

Of course it is possible to over-emphasize contradic-tions within the Bible, but it is also possible to resolve them too slickly. The variety of contradictions of the Bible can be held together only if one has an over-all view of the Scriptures as witnessing, sometimes in very frag-mentary and partial ways to the character and purpose of God. Such a standpoint is reflected in the great book *Doxology*, where Geoffrey Wainwright uses the phrase 'the variegated unity of the Bible'.[2]

25

Lectionaries and Scripture

Lectionaries exist in order to witness to the manifold character of God that we find in the Scriptures, and to ensure the systematic reading of the Bible. Almost invariably they involve a principle of selection. There have probably been few times in which the *whole* Bible was in *practice* read in public worship. When Thomas Cranmer appointed the Old Testament to be read through every year he added the rider 'except certain bokes and chapiters, which bee least edifying, and might best be spared, and therefore are left unred'. Similarly, although in his first Prayer Book he intended the New Testament to be read thrice in the year, he seems to have been less smitten with Revelation than are the compilers of modern lectionaries. By common consent and usage, certain passages are never read in worship. Nevertheless, at a parish *pardon* in Brittany some twenty-five years ago, Matthew 1.1 – 17 was read both in Latin and in French – presumably to evoke a sense of history and of God's purpose running through it!

Lectionaries are beset by two dangers. In the first place, they can make for a wooden and mechanical reading of Scripture. Of their nature they cannot allow for particular needs, circumstances and congregations. The daily lectionary for Matins and Evensong in the Church of England is probably not widely used outside the ranks of the clergy. But there is an exception in cathedrals and choral foundations which often attract visitors whose connection with the Church may be slender. On an autumn Saturday afternoon in every other year, Nahum 1 is read; but can it mean anything without a fair bit of background information, and would that information justify its use in *public* worship? Or does Acts 7, split up into four sections, make very appropriate *New* Testament lessons? Such examples could be multiplied.

On the other hand if we restrict readings – even in the

26

interests of cathedral visitors – to what could be described as 'relevant' or 'meaningful' it is hard to know where the process would end, and fairly certain that the resultant lectionary would no longer witness to the manifold character of God that is disclosed in the Scriptures. Progress in the Christian faith means a willingness to go on learning – a theological student had to be reminded of this when he said that the second lesson at Evensong (2 Corinthians 4!) meant nothing to him. Moreover, what one generation rejects, the next sometimes rediscovers. When our forefathers used the Venite, they meant the whole of Psalm 95. The 1928 revisers of the Prayer Book appointed only the first seven verses as an appropriate introduction to worship. Some biblical scholars pointed out that the remaining verses were integral to the Psalm, and quoted extensively in the letter to the Hebrews. The ASB Venite is therefore a composite canticle, certainly including 'today' and a verse of Psalm 96 as well.

Neville Clark sums up the dilemma as follows:

> A mechanistic use of scripture is unjustifiable. Each paragraph or chapter is not a unit of exactly equal weight with every other, nor does the absence of some sections necessarily distort the whole. Yet the road of selection remains a perilous path beset by a host of unbiblical spirits whose leaders are named Arbitrariness and Subjectivity, and probably no lectionary survives entirely unscathed. [3]

So far we have been looking at the daily lectionary for Matins and Evensong in the Church of England. It is time to turn to that which is more widely known – the eucharistic lectionary for Sundays. Both lectionaries are, in fact, ecumenical in inspiration. They are based on work done in the sixties by the Joint Liturgical Group, with the result that the lectionaries of The Alternative Service Book, The Methodist Service Book, the Book of Common

Order and a Book of Services (URC) differ only occasionally in detail. The main difference lies in the fact that whereas the lectionary is *prescribed* in the Church of England, it is *recommended* in the other churches mentioned above.

The basic presupposition of the lectionary is that of Thomas Cranmer – namely that it is desirable that the worshipping community on Sundays should hear as wide a selection as possible from the scriptures. For that reason, the lectionary is spread over two years and three readings are appointed – from the Old Testament, the gospels and other parts of the New Testament – as well as a selection of psalmody. The three lessons are linked by a very broad theme, so that the choice of one lesson suggests the choice of the other two. The first is sometimes called the 'controlling' lesson inasmuch as it 'controls' the choice of the others. In the nine Sundays before Christmas where the emphasis is on the world's preparation for Christ, this 'controlling' lesson is from the Old Testament; in the period between Christmas and Pentecost where the emphasis is on the life and ministry of Christ, it is from the gospels; and in the period after Pentecost where the emphasis is on our life in the Spirit it is from the epistles, Acts or Revelation. The general themes are listed in the ASB and other service books. Their place in the framing and use of the Anglican Lectionary is described in the official commentary to the ASB:

> It cannot be too strongly emphasized that scripture is primary, and must be allowed to speak for itself, whilst the themes set out in the table are secondary and provided only as 'guides for those who wish to use them'. In framing the table of readings, the passages from the Bible which ought to be read were first selected, and only then were they ordered and given sequence so that some general progression

emerged. The Joint Liturgical Group insisted that the thematic titles are no more than indications of emphasis, and must not be allowed to give false rigidity to the hearing of scripture and the preaching of the Word of God.[4]

C. S. Lewis once wrote of a parson who had twenty favourite lessons and fifteen favourite psalms. It is the purpose of a lectionary to protect everyone from such a limited choice. Nevertheless, there are other questions to be asked about lectionaries in general and the one we have been describing in particular, and to these we now turn.

Four questions about lectionaries

1. Is contemporary worship too biblical?
The Dean of Worcester argues very strongly that it is.[5] Others would sympathize with his view that two readings are sufficient in the Eucharist. But he believes that the gospel is 'rightly mandatory'. Yet modern critical scholarship sees as much 'gospel' in the epistles as in the four evangelists, and if we insist that one of the two passages read must be from the gospels, it means a very thin spread for the rest of the Bible. The newcomer to the Anglican liturgy is, of course, the Old Testament lesson. This can be strongly defended on grounds of antiquity (certainly used in the early Church) and of theology (a necessary background to the New Testament), and it is certainly true that as many people's church attendance is confined to the Eucharist, this is their only chance of hearing the Old Testament. Geoffrey Wainwright suggests that 'the absence of the Old Testament brings into relief the radical "newness" of the Christian message' but still comes down in favour of its inclusion.[6]

In fact, the total number of verses appointed for a Sunday service averages 30–40; this is not excessive, and would probably not seem so if the verses in *two* readings amounted to this number. But the Dean of Worcester may be on surer ground when he complains that the services are peppered with texts and allusions totally lifted from context. He was writing of the Series 3 service, but the ASB has made further provision of texts to be used at the beginning of the service and after communion. The selection seems to bear the marks of haste; can

> Abraham is the Father of all: as Scripture says 'I have made you the father of many nations'

be invariably appropriate as an opening of worship on the seventh Sunday before Christmas?

2. Is there too little interpretation of Scripture?

It is neither possible nor desirable that everything read in a service should be explained; the result would be insupportably tedious and didactic. But to the question 'Should there be introductions to lessons?', the answer surely is 'sometimes'. Bishop Michael Marshall argues very strongly against this when he says 'the word of God in formal worship must be allowed to speak for itself' and goes on,

> The Scriptures do not primarily call to be explained; they demand first and before all else to be obeyed. [7]

Nevertheless it can help people to know who Micah was, and what the letter to the Hebrews sets out to do; for these writings have their own context, and they can speak to us more effectively if we know how they spoke of old. When such introductions are used, the greatest care must be taken over their compilation. The reader must not preach another sermon, nor must he pre-empt the forthcoming sermon. On the other hand, if the introduction merely says something like 'a call to faith' it is as well left unsaid.

There is no dearth of books offering material for introductions to readings. [8]

3. What about omissions from the lectionary?

The present lectionary, as we have seen, provides for 104 Sundays. The Roman Catholic Church, whose representatives participated in the discussions of the Joint Liturgical Group, has extended its principles further in providing a three-year scheme of readings. But always there are omissions. Here is one perhaps rather odd example.

The writer once preached a sermon on Balaam. He was in good company, as two great nineteenth century preachers – J. H. Newman and F. W. Robertson – did the same thing. But the story does not crop up in the eucharistic lectionary. It would not be safe to assume that congregation knew it; to tell the story before preaching about it would be either tedious or lame or both. The simplest solution would be to allow a preacher to choose a reading alternative to that appointed *provided such a reading did not occur elsewhere in the two-year cycle.* This would ensure both discipline and freedom. Such permission would protect us from incessant use of Isaiah 6.1 – 8 on the one hand, but allow the possibility of Balaam on the other.

The lectionary ought not to be a strait-jacket. As Neville Clark writes:

> The preacher must remember that the total canon of Scripture imposes itself for his plundering and the congregation must recognise that the restricting of the use of Scripture to the confines of the litugical assembly is a recipe for immaturity. [9]

4. Is there a place for non-biblical readings?

There seems a strong case for such. It seems hard to believe that the inspiration of the Holy Spirit ended with the closing of the canon of Scripture, or that passages from St Augustine, Jeremy Taylor or Dietrich Bonhoeffer would not be more edifying than the battles of David or those of the Maccabean period. But there are problems connected on the one hand with the authority of Scripture, and on the other with the subjectivity that the choice of such passages would entail. They have an obvious place in extra-liturgical services on special occasions. Sometimes they could be regarded as a commentary upon Scripture and presented as such. If this sort of commentary were added to the three lessons, it would require a high degree of skill and sensitivity on the part of those preparing and leading worship, with the sermon and perhaps other parts of the liturgy adjusted so that time and balance were not overthrown.

Presenting the Bible in worship

> The Bible to many is both too well known and too little; it lacks the charm of novelty on the one hand, and is not deeply loved and cherished on the other. [10]

So writes Christina Le Moignan. If this is true, it means that great care must be taken, without over-dramatization, to ensure that the freshness and vitality of the Scriptures is not diminished, and that they are not read as if they were a seed catalogue.

In the first place, this means good individual readers. When clergy seek to involve or honour the laity, they often do so by inviting them to read lessons. At a civic service, perhaps, the Mayor is asked to read. He is not asked to sing a solo because it is by no means certain that he is able to do so. But it is assumed that everyone is capable of reading aloud in public – whereas this is as much an art as singing. In most parishes, we cannot restrict the lessons to the best readers; but a willingness to learn and to practise goes some way to ensuring that the reader will give the best of which he or she is capable. If the choir practises, so should the lesson readers.

Some passages lend themselves to more than one voice. The dramatic reading of the passion by several voices is now common in many churches. In many passages dialogue is effective. The fourth servant song (Isaiah 52.13 – 53; 12) is one example. Christina Le Moignan suggests similar treatment for James 4.1 – 10; one reader takes the 'accusing verses', 1 – 5, a second reads the 'gospel offer', verses 6 – 8a, and they join to read the call to repentance in verses 8b – 10. In the same article she suggests the occasional use of visual accompaniments or sound effects after the fashion of television and radio programmes. All this requires the most thorough preparation, but mention of TV and radio immediately points the contrast between the care with which programmes are compiled and the casual or slipshod preparations for public worship.

Some sections of the Bible cannot easily be broken up into short 'lessons'. Job is arguably better read at a single sitting or perhaps three. Walton probably makes *Belshazzar's Feast* live more than reading can do -- but not every church has a choral society able to perform it. Yet many churches could introduce simple music, drama or dance, and there could be services at which there was extended reading of some part of the Bible interspersed with comment, singing and prayers – rather like the 'nine lessons' at Christmas except that all nine might be from the same book.

It is not the function of this chapter to discuss Bible study groups or similar activities. It is generally true that, excellent as they may be, they attract only a minority of our congregations. It is therefore necessary that there should be, within the context of *public* worship, as wide and varied a presentation of the Bible as possible – certainly in the hope that interest will be so aroused as to

33

encourage its further study by individuals and in groups. And in all such presentations, there must be regard not only for what is effective but for what the Scriptures actually say. Preachers are taught to be scrupulous about the meaning of texts; so must all who seek to present the message of the Bible.

Variety of presentation involves variety of response. Wooden faces are not necessarily a sign of reverence. One of the differences between a theological college and a cathedral is that in the latter, people seldom laugh during lessons. But there is humour in the Bible as well as gravity, and hilarity is not incompatible with seriousness. Both contribute attention, and both may be involved in response.

The reading and hearing of the word matter. As Origen wrote:

> You who are accustomed to be present at the divine mysteries know how you receive the Lord's body with every care and reverence . . . if you use and rightly use such care about his body, why do you think it less of a crime to be negligent about his word ?[11]

Notes

1. Quiller Couch, *On the Art of Reading*, CUP, Pocket Edition, 1924, pp. 154 – 156.
2. Geoffrey Wainwright, *Doxology*, Epworth Press, 1980, pp. 169 – 175.
3. Neville Clark, 'The Bible and the Liturgy' in *Getting the Liturgy Right* (ed. R. C. D. Jasper), SPCK, 1982, pp. 27 – 28.
4. Church Information Office, *The Alternative Service Book: A Commentary by the Liturgical Commission*, 1980, p.30.
5. T. G. A. Baker, *Questioning Worship*, SCM Press, 1977, pp. 20 – 33.
6. Wainwright, op. cit., pp. 173 – 174.

7. Michael Marshall, *Renewal in Worship*, Marshall, Morgan & Scott, 1982, p.125.

8. Amongst them, those printed by Mowbray and Epworth Press. *The Ministry of the Word* (ed. G. Cuming), BRF/OUP, 1979, is a quarry of material for such.

9. Clark, op. cit., p.28.

10. Christina Le Moignan, *Worship and Preaching*, Vol. 13 No.3.

11. Quoted in Wainwright, op. cit., p.180.

4. THE GOD WHO SPEAKS TO US

'Of making many books there is no end', says Ecclesi-
astes, and in some theological fields, the flow turns into a
flood. This is certainly true of commentaries on St John's
gospel, and it is also true of books on preaching. The last
four years have seen the publication of *The Ministry of the
Word*, perhaps the *magnum opus* of Douglas Cleverley
Ford, so long the Director of the College of Preachers in
the Church of England; a new book on preaching by John
Stott and a reassessment of it by John Stacey; *A Handbook
of Parish Preaching* together with Grove Pamphlets and
articles in various journals; two very useful books that
seek to relate critical biblical scholarship to the
preparation of sermons;[1] and the continued publication
of collections of sermons and sermon outlines. The spate
of books suggests that people still care about preaching
and want to know something about it. This is one reason
why its place in worship deserves a chapter in this book.

The authority of preaching

Our God speaks to us. The God of the Bible is invariably
seeking to communicate with men and women. The story
of the Bible is the story of how such communication is
made.

Douglas Cleverley Ford asserts:

> Israel heard preaching late in her history. She en-
> countered it on the lips of prophets who did not
> make an appearance until the ninth century BC, a
> time when the nation's faith and worship had grown
> and developed.[2]

36

But when preaching arrived, it stayed. By New Testament times, people spoke of 'the law and the prophets' as though the two were equal in value. With all the variety to be found amongst the great Hebrew prophets, they seem to have had a common fourfold aim: (1) to expose the evil of the times, (2) to proclaim its consequences, (3) to recall people to the nature of their God, and (4) to call for a change of heart. Their message was prefaced by 'Thus saith the Lord' or (NEB) 'This is the very word of the Lord'.

Obviously, the prophets do not mark the beginning of communication. Ezra the scribe had stood on a platform and read the Law to the people – it took a few hours. The Authorized Version calls the platform 'a pulpit of wood' which tells us more about the religion of the seventeenth century than that of Ezra. The origins of preaching go back beyond the prophets. Yet the prophets brought a new dimension to the religion of their generation. 'Thus saith the Lord' sums up the authority of their message; they are seen as his spokesmen; and God comes to be described quaintly as one who 'rises up early' and sends his prophets.

If preaching came late in the life of Hebrew religion as it was before Christ, Christianity was born with it. A sermon was regularly preached in the synagogue, and when Jesus returned to Nazareth after his baptism, he was invited to preach one. So was Paul when he got to Antioch. It is likely that this custom from the synagogue was transferred to the meetings for Christians in private houses; the worship in house churches today may be very different from the formal atmosphere of a church, but usually still bears some relation to it. One such meeting is recorded (Acts 20) in Troas on a Saturday night when people met for the breaking of the bread. On that occasion Paul preached a very long sermon; and the detail has been preserved because a young man got so drowsy that he fell from the third storey to the ground.

It is another sort of preaching that is recorded in the New Testament. This was the proclamation of the basic facts about Jesus and their significance to those who had never heard or believed them. This might happen in a friendly synagogue, or, more often, in the open air. Humanly speaking, it was to such preaching that the Christian Church owed its early and dramatic expansion.

R. H. Fuller[3] finds three kinds of preaching discernible in the New Testament. The first is *kerygma* – proclamation to the unconverted. The second is *paraklesis* – renewal and deepening of the *kerygma*. The third is *didache* – instruction of the new converts, the recently baptized in Christian ethics and doctrine. It would be unwise to draw too sharp a distinction between these three. The 'unconverted' at least shared the apostles' belief in God and the promise of the Messiah, and had to be persuaded that the Messiah had come: and there were doubtless those who only half understood what they had heard. Christian communication today may similarly be divided. There is the presentation in public worship which involves some kind of renewal of those basic truths; and there is straightforward instruction which normally happens outside formal liturgy and often in small groups. Again, the distinctions are useful, but must not be exaggerated. We are still likely to have amongst regular worshippers some who have never really grasped what it is about; and proclamation and instruction often shade into one another. But this is to jump ahead, and we must look at our inheritance of preaching.

The tradition of preaching

It would seem, then, from the scanty evidence available, that preaching was from earliest days a normal part of the programme for the Christian assembly at worship as well as being the only available method of presenting the gospel to unbelievers. Justin Martyr's description of the Sunday morning service in Rome at about AD 140 is the earliest and fullest account of Christian worship after the New Testament documents. He tells us that before the breaking of the bread there were readings from the prophets and the memoirs of the apostles 'so far as time allows', and that this was followed by a discourse from the president. Preaching remained in theory an integral part of the Eucharist, though the evidence suggests that in the late Middle Ages it was no longer regular and normal, and that the open-air sermons of the friars were certainly more popular.

The Reformation itself gave preaching the prominent place it was to have in all the Churches deriving from it. Martin Luther's rediscovery of the Word had to be proclaimed by word. In Zurich, Zwingli's week-by-week exposition of Scripture after Mass was as important for the reformation of liturgy as it was for doctrine. It has often been pointed out that after the Reformation the ear became more important than the eye for the worshipper. The new importance of preaching was reflected in the arrangement of churches. Some churches of the Reformation began to place the pulpit where the altar had once been — so that all could see the preacher, and the preacher could see all. Sometimes in eighteenth century Anglican churches, the altar was left in its traditional place in an empty chancel for the quarterly administration of the Sacrament, and the nave dominated by a three-decker pulpit. In Canterbury Cathedral, the congregation at one time resorted to the chapter house for the sermon — where it could be heard in greater comfort!

Sermons were held in high esteem by all kinds of Protestants. Obviously they meant more to the Evangelical kinds of Christians; but it is significant that the Oxford Movement with its strong sacramental and liturgical emphasis was popularized by the sermons of Newman in Oxford and later by such men as Church and Liddon at St

Paul's. The sermon was no less important to those eighteenth century theologians whose aim was a non-dogmatic moral religion. Geoffrey Wainwright has an amusing description of sermons in Germany after the Enlightenment. Easter Monday's sermon, based on the story of Emmaus, could be about 'going for walks'. 'Stealing wood' was recommended as a subject for the first Sunday in Advent when the gospel recorded the cutting down of branches to strew at the feet of Jesus.[4] The pulpit was unhesitatingly used for the propagation of political views. On hearing of the death of Queen Anne, a preacher chose the text 'Go, bury this accursed woman; for she is a king's daughter'. A thunderous utterance of the famous Victorian preacher Joseph Parker in the City Temple ended with the words 'God damn the Sultan'.

We must not linger on such curiosities. But at the beginning of this century, it looked as though Protestant worship centred around the pulpit and Catholic worship around the altar, with the Anglican tradition swinging a bit between the two. This is of course a wide generalization which ignores such historical features as the sacramental emphasis of the Wesleys or the importance of the missionary preaching of the Jesuits for the Roman Catholic Church. But in 1938, Karl Barth wrote:

> What we know today as the church service both in Roman Catholicism and in Protestantism is a torso. The Roman Catholic Church has a sacramental service without preaching. We have a service with a sermon without sacraments. Both types of service are impossible.[5]

Barth lived long enough to see the beginnings of change. Through the ecumenical and liturgical movements, through the World Council of Churches and Vatican 2, through a growing together that was not always planned or engineered, there has come a new evaluation of preaching in the Roman Catholic Church and a new evaluation of the sacraments in the Churches of the Reformation. A sermon or homily is normal and expected at Sunday Mass in the Roman Catholic Church. The same is true of Parish Communion in the Church of England. In the English Free Churches, Communion is not only observed more frequently, but more often within a regular service than as an adjunct to it. The twin importance of word and sacrament has become a theological and liturgical commonplace.

Alternatives to Preaching

But although the place of the sermon is sure in modern liturgies and its importance is stressed by modern liturgists, it has declined in popular estimation during the present century. In the decade that preceded the First World War, many Nonconformist churches had a preaching service during the week; in one such it was held on a *Monday* evening, and much looked forward to by women who had slaved all day over the copper and the mangle. A weekday Evensong with sermon was also by no means uncommon in urban Anglican churches.

The sermon is no longer given a very high rating as entertainment. This is one quite important reason for its decline. It did have such value (even though preachers might pooh-pooh the idea), and there were many who played up to it. But now entertainment is available in the home at the push of a knob. Nor do sermons have the educational value that they held in days when people were less literate and less articulate. If preaching were seriously offered as a means of instruction, it would contradict almost every modern educational method.

These are but two of the reasons why sermons no longer

hold that sway that was theirs for nearly four hundred years. There are those who think it has had its day. They would say that dialogue is more acceptable than monologue, and that for most people the visual is again more effective than the oral. They would point to all the techniques of film and transparency, and ask why a preacher still stands six feet above contradiction – or even at one of the little lecterns now considered more suitable for preaching.

This chapter will make a case for preaching – with the writer's belief that it has an important role – provided that this role is more narrowly defined. Many things that used to be done through preaching can now better be done by other means, and we will briefly consider some of these.

The first kind of preaching classified by R. H. Fuller was the proclamation of the gospel to those who had never heard it, or never believed it. The modern equivalent might be open-air preaching as in Hyde Park. It still happens, and it may still have a place. But if we want to reach people where they are, we are more likely to use the media; and, if we use the media, we are likely to use more than one voice and more than one scene. So this will not be preaching in the accepted sense of the word. Fuller's third category was *didache*, teaching. This is more likely to happen in house-churches, Bible study groups or confirmation classes. And again, this will not be by means of monologue, and it is not likely in any way to resemble preaching.

But what of that second category of preaching that Fuller described as the renewal and deepening of the *kerygma*: the kind of preaching that we seem to find described by Justin Martyr? Once again this can happen through music, through poetry and through dance and movement. But for most people the value of such methods lies partly in their novelty or occasional use. Moreover it would require an organization more numerous and more wealthy than we find in most of our churches to provide such a programme week by week.

So the sermon remains the staple diet. It does not seek to do what can be done better by other methods, but rather to do something in its own right. It is not a means of purveying information, though it may well tell some people some things that they did not know before. It is not an opportunity for a preacher to tell his congregation his own views on all current matters of debate – though there may be times when the preacher who has prayed and searched the scriptures must say with Martin Luther 'Here I stand: I can no other'.

The role of preaching

What then is preaching? Many excellent definitions have been offered, but here is a simple one. Preaching is a means whereby the words of the Bible become the word of God to those who listen. A fairly radical theologian used to preface his sermon with the aspiration (not quite a prayer, because it was not quite clear to whom it was addressed) 'May I speak and you hear the word of God'.

This sort of sermon makes at least three demands on the preacher. First, he must really get to grips with the passage or text that he seeks to interpret. It is not enough to have a vague impression of what it says; and many a conscientious preacher has had to change direction in preparing his sermon because he found the text did not mean quite what he thought it meant when he first chose it. Sermon preparation requires prayer and study; and this must be a priority for the preacher. Secondly he must keep in touch with the world in which he lives – being alert to the media, the novel, his own pastoral concerns and what is revealed to him through any work in which he is engaged. If, for example, he uses the word 'nowadays' (experience suggests that it is a rather dangerous word in the pulpit) he must be sure that it really is 'nowadays' to which he alludes, and not some day of the past or one of his own imagination. Thirdly he must be concerned about how the first can be related to the second, and more particularly how to present his message so that what he wants to say is that which is actually heard by the congregation. This means that he will not disdain voice-training and re-training; that he will try to develop a style that is lively but not histrionic; that he will search for the right words, the right length for sentences, the proper times to pause; and that he will seek illustrations that do illustrate his message, and reject others (however entertaining) that will detract from the attention of the hearers.

We must not delve too deeply into sermon techniques, for this book is not intended solely for preachers. Nor does it want to maintain the common impression that preaching is mainly the business of preachers. Preachers are made by congregations, and a congregation must be prepared for the ministry of the word. It must in the first place be expectant – waiting for the word of God that is to be given. It must be quiet. Unwrapping of sweet papers really can distract those sitting nearby, especially when people think they are unwrapping them quietly. More seriously, the presence of the very young however welcome, can create enormous problems both for preachers and congregations. The quesion is large and the area highly sensitive; suffice it to say here that if facilities allow, it does seem desirable that the very young should be taken out during an adult sermon which parents might take it in turns to attend. For a congregation must also be attentive; this is never easy, but important unless all sermons are recorded and can be played back again. And a congregation must remember that you do not have to agree with everything said in a sermon in order to derive some benefit from it.

There is a story that when chaplains preached before King George V, he asked for the text on Saturday night so that he also could think about it before the sermon was delivered. For Anglicans the printing of the readings in the ASB (like the epistle and gospel in the BCP) gives members of the congregation the chance to do something that is invaluable for their own preparation – namely to read through the passages themselves at home.

The position of the sermon in Rites A and B suggests that it should be in some sense expository, and in most other liturgies it is similarly placed directly after the readings. A strong dissentient voice is raised by the Dean of Worcester,[6] but alongside his plea for less directly biblical preaching is the suggestion that there might be an organ voluntary between gospel and readings. Most people think otherwise; but whereas some would want to start with the Bible and proceed to apply its message to their hearers, others would want to start with some aspect of the human situation, and then see what light the Bible throws upon it. A wise preacher is likely sometimes to use the one method and at other times the second, aiming at as varied a presentation as possible. The sermon is not meant to be stereotyped. But the bright comment on yesterday's football match or last week's television programme can become as hackneyed as the question, 'What does Paul mean by that?'. And congregations who expect illumination from the Bible are not likely to be switched off by a sermon that comes fairly quickly to its message.

We have noted that most modern liturgies see a direct relationship between the breaking of the word and the breaking of the bread. The two activities belong to each other. Both are designed to bring the things of the past into the present – to show that the God who acted in history is the God who acts now. When Jesus said, 'Do this in remembrance of me', he did not mean that when we break bread in worship we should simply remember that he once did the same. Remembrance, as biblical scholarship of this century has been at great pains to point out, has far richer connotations; remembrance makes the

45

saving activity of God, as recorded in history, real to us now. It is set forth symbolically in the eucharistic action, and verbally in the sermon. The sermon will always – however indirectly -- help us to enter into the mystery of redemption as expressed in the eucharistic action; and that action will therefore be a kind of embodiment of the word that has been preached.

If preaching is seen in this way, it does not lend itself to public discussion. That would be rather like discussing the quality of the communion wine. Of course people may want to talk to one another about it; they may want to talk in groups, they may want to talk to the preacher. But discussion requires a setting that is different from the sermon. People's expectation is different, for one thing; the chairs or seating must be differently arranged, for another. Many subjects, biblical and doctrinal as well as ethical and liturgical, do lend themselves to discussion, and certainly ought to be discussed. That could even happen during worship, but it would be a different sort of worship, because this is a different sort of activity. This brings us back to the point stressed earlier in this chapter. There are many forms of communication, and some are more adequate for tasks which the sermon used to fulfil; but the value of the sermon is best appreciated if its unique, narrow and deep character is understood.

On a practical level, there are, of course, difficulties. It is hard to get the people of God together for an hour on Sundays, let alone at any other time. 'They won't come to anything else', is the frequent and justified moan of the clergy. If this is totally irreversible, then we need fresh thought about how that hour should be spent. But most people who have taken part in small informal gatherings testify that they have experienced through them something that cannot be found in the more formal assembly. Bible study groups and house groups do and can grow.

One of the most recent books on preaching mentioned at the opening of this chapter asks the question, 'Is preaching all it is made out to be?'[7] The author who is among other things, connexional Local Preachers' Secretary in the Methodist Church comes to the somewhat un-Methodist conclusion that it is not. He does not think that preaching in practice corresponds to the high claims made for it by such theologians as Karl Barth, P. T. Forsyth and H. H. Farmer. But perhaps the most important thing stressed in Stacey's book is the need for modesty:

> Modesty, like humility, of which it is a part, simply rests in a true identity, not a false one.[8]

This chapter has sought to recover the true identity of preaching. The writer takes a high view of preaching, seeing it as the breaking of the word and analogous to the breaking of the bread. Its role is unique and lofty, but it must not arrogate to itself that which does not belong to itself:

> A good sermon is one rooted in the Bible, interpreted for the twentieth century, finding its ratification in the tradition and experience of the Church and the preacher's own experience, and evoking the kind of Christian Faith that has an easy relevance to the daily lives of its hearers.[9]

Perhaps this seems far removed from Richard Baxter:

> I preached as never sure to preach again,
> And as a dying man, to dying men.

But it may simply mean that we want to combine conviction with openness, confidence with humility. Preachers may long to have lived in the age of Donne or Newman or Sangster. But that is not our age. Yet, as God still uses the simple elements of bread and wine to make his love and power known to us, so he uses the aspirations and short-comings of preachers to make his word heard.

Notes

1. Donald E. Gowan, *Reclaiming the Old Testament for the Christian Pulpit*, T & T Clark, 1981. Eric Franklin, *How the Critics can Help*, SCM, 1982.
2. D. W. Cleverley Ford, *The Ministry of the Word*, Hodder & Stoughton, 1979, p.28.
3. R. H. Fuller, *What is Liturgical Preaching?*, SCM, 1957, p.22.
4. Geoffrey Wainwright, *Doxology*, Epworth, 1980, p.333.
5. Karl Barth, *The Knowledge of God and the Service of God*, quoted in Fuller, op. cit., p.13.
6. T. G. A. Baker, *Questioning Worship*, SCM, 1977, p.32.
7. John Stacey, *Preaching Reassessed*, Epworth, 1980.
8. Stacey, op. cit., p.125.
9. Stacey, op. cit., p.22.

5. THE GOD WHO LISTENS TO US

The God who speaks to us is also the God who listens to us. We have more than once insisted that the God of the Scriptures is constantly seeking to communicate with men and women; it would be more accurate and more biblical to say that he is always in relationship with them. This relationship is focussed in prayer.

Prayer in the Bible

The second part of Genesis begins with the story of Abraham. It tells us that Abraham who listens to the voice of God and obeys it also speaks with God – as on the celebrated occasion where he pleads for the righteous in Sodom. In Exodus, after the description of the tent of the presence, the writer says 'The Lord would speak with Moses face to face as one man speaks to another'. The text implies, though it does not state, that there was dialogue, and we have many examples of times when Moses spoke to the Lord. These conversations are surely not meant to be understood in a crude and literal way, but rather as pointers to the depth of relationship possible between God and human beings. Indeed there are descriptions of subtle and varied ways in which this relationship is experienced by people; angels and dreams may seem just part of an ancient culture, but are indicative of the diversity of ways in which communication takes place.

When we get to the dedication of Solomon's temple, we hear something about public and ceremonial prayer. Solomon says 'Hear the supplications of thy servant and thy people Israel when they pray towards this place. Hear thou in heaven thy dwelling, and when thou hearest, forgive.' 1 Kings 8 details a number of circumstances which will bring people to prayer, and to supplication for forgiveness.

The New Testament provides us with a variety of illustrations of Christian prayer. These were listed with commentary some years ago in a book by Archbishop Coggan,[1] and from the same period came a useful book called *Jewish Prayer and Worship.*[2] A public prayer is set out in full in Acts 4.24–31 after Peter and John had been brought before the Sanhedrin. Peter begins by recalling what God has done in the past, and continues 'Stretch out thy hand to heal, and cause signs and wonders to be done through the name of thy holy servant Jesus'.

Prayer seems from earliest times to have been an indispensable part of Christian worship, as it was for the Jews. At Philippi there was apparently no synagogue, but Paul and his friends sought out a place where prayer was offered – that is, in all probability a spot in the open air where Jews gathered on the Sabbath (Acts 16.11–17). It is evident and hardly surprising that the prayers of the early Christian community were heavily influenced by Jewish prayer. But at the beginning of 1 Timothy 2, the writer set out some features that ought to be characteristic of the prayers of the assembly:

> First of all, then, I urge that petitions, prayers, intercessions and thanksgivings be offered for all men; for sovereigns and all in high office, that we may lead a tranquil and quiet life in full observance of religion and high standards of morality. Such prayer is right and approved by God our Saviour, whose will it is that all men should find salvation and come to know the truth.

The Book of Common Prayer provides plenty of prayers

for the sovereign, so that is one part of the New Testament which it took seriously.

To return to the more general point: in Acts 2.42 we are told of the young Christian community 'They met constantly to hear the apostles teach, and to share the common life, to break bread, and to pray'. When Justin Martyr (to whom reference has been made in the last chapter) had described the readings and the sermon he added, 'After this we all rise at once and offer prayers'. He surely intended no double meaning.

Let us pray

Older liturgies were plentifully seasoned with this exhortation. It meant precisely what it said. But it is not so interpreted. It is commonly taken as a command to change posture. Anglicans will therefore kneel, or, more often, adopt a posture midway between sitting and kneeling. Free Church congregations are likely to bend forward. Roman Catholics seem unaffected. One of the first things that Anglican leaders of worship have to learn is that they must not say 'Let us pray' if they do not want the congregation to move. There was a catch in the old Prayer Book Marriage Service. The priest said 'Let us pray' but the rubric directed that only the bridegroom and bride should kneel. The priest had therefore to choose between omitting the injunction altogether, or engaging in what could be a wordy explanation as to why the rest of the congregation should remain standing.

We have moved to some peripheral but quite important considerations affecting the planning and practice of public prayer.

1. Posture
In his terrible caricature of a sermon preached during

the 1914 – 18 war, Geoffrey Studdert Kennedy quoted a
preacher thus:[3]

> Our shrieks of pain go up in vain,
> The wide world's miseries
> Must still persist, until we learn
> To pray upon our knees.
>
> Upon our knees, my friends, I said,
> And mark well what I say,
> God wants to see us on our knees,
> The proper place to pray.

We have moved a long way from those days when
people supposed that one posture and one only was appropriate for prayer. We know that in the Christian world –
let alone among religions in general – a variety of posture
has been and is observed. Standing has increased in popularity in the West (it has always been common in the
East), and 'too much standing' is sometimes a complaint
about newer services. Standing is still a mark of respect in
our society, and standing to receive communion could be
understood as such. Or it could be seen as a symbol of the
status which God has conferred upon us as a redeemed
people and forgiven sinners, whereas kneeling could be a
sign of our need for forgiveness. Both things are true of
us, for, as Martin Luther reminded us, we are both sinful
and justified.

If a variety of posture is admitted, there would seem a
case for standing to praise and thank God, kneeling for
confession and intercession, and sitting for the kind of
prayer that is meditative. The Alternative Service Book
wisely indicates when a certain posture is appropriate, but
with equal wisdom adds 'for the rest, local custom may be
established and followed'. We might add that it is by no
means essential for everyone in the congregation to do the
same – though the fear of being conspicuous makes this
hard for most people to take.

2. Style

Not so long ago Christians in these islands seemed divided between those who adhered rigidly to a book for worship and those who were violently opposed to such. We have moved a long way from that situation. In the Free Churches, it is by no means uncommon to find at least some of the prayers read; in the Anglican eucharistic liturgy, there is one point (the intercessions) where freer prayer is encouraged — as it is in the Roman rite. The arguments can be briefly summarized. Written prayers, it is claimed, when habitually used, can give a sense of stability, a framework into which private prayer can be inserted; but, it is sometimes alleged, their very familiarity can have an effect that is deadening, formal and perfunctory. Prayers newly composed can have a positive freshness and vitality — but they can quickly become stereotyped and hackneyed. In Howard Spring's novel, *Fame is the Spur*, there was a character called Birley Artingstall who on Sundays

> might be found in the Emmott Street Wesleyan Chapel enduring everything patiently: anthem and hymns, sermon and announcements and collection, waiting for the prayer-meeting that followed the evening service. It was for the moment when the Minister would say 'Perhaps Brother Birley Artingstall will lead us to the mercy-seat' that Birley lived. The tall drooping length of him would stand, one hand grasping the end of his pew, the other clenching and unclenching spasmodically, and out of him would pour petitions that once had the virtue of extemporaneous utterance, but now were polished and rehearsed litanies. His voice began with cool and reasonable suggestions to a Deity not beyond the reach of common sense, and gathered in a few dutiful Amens. Stage by stage it reached at last a thunderous utterance which culminated invariably in a

command to the Lord to come quickly and 'sway the
sceptre of universal dominion'. The fervent 'Hal-
lelujahs' that fell like bouquets around Birley
Artingstall as he sat down made all but the most
obdurate hesitant to follow him. He was always
pathetically anxious and restless once the prayer-
meeting had broken up, until someone had said to
him 'You led us tonight with great acceptance'.[4]

That quotation – or diversion – may seem to lead the
arguments one way, but in fact they are equally balanced,
and most modern liturgies find room for both styles of
prayer. But it is wise to bear in mind Isaac Watts' distinction between 'free' and 'extemporary' prayer.

Free or 'conceived' prayer is prepared before the
service; it is done by some work of meditation before
we begin to speak in prayer. Extemporary prayer is
spontaneous and unpremeditated – when we without any reflection or meditation beforehand address
ourselves to God and speak the thoughts of our
hearts as fast as we can conceive them.[5]

Generally speaking the former method will be more appropriate in public worship and more acceptable as *common* prayer. It can help leaders to bring freshness into
prayer, and protect them from the temptations of Birley
Artingstall. Watts' further admonition to ministers of his
own Congregational tradition would still be appropriate
for those who lead prayers. For he advocated avoiding

these two extremes (i) of confining ourselves to pre-
composed forms of prayer (ii) an entire dependence
on sudden motions and suggestions of thought.[6]

3. *Language*
When the current edition of *New Every Morning* was

54

published in 1973, Archbishop Michael Ramsey wrote succinctly in the foreword:

> Is prayer in modern English a good thing? If the language is self-consciously modern and full of jargon and cliché, No. But if the language is simple and natural, Yes. [7]

The battle over language is not waged so fiercely as it was (in some quarters) in 1973, but Ramsey's words still need to be heeded by those who compose prayers. He had earlier made some criticisms of the English Prayer Book tradition as being 'too verbose, too preachy and too cerebral'. Certainly it is so – in parts – though many of the collects show an admirable economy of words. But it has its equals. As late as 1940, a suggested order of intercession in the Scottish Book of Common Order contained the lines:

> Maintain and increase the noble estate of the Queen's majesty, her royal house, her ministers and counsellors and the whole body of the Commonwealth.

In marked contrast were the (often) one-line forms of intercession and meditation devised by George Appleton, surely one of the most skilful and sensitive composers of prayer in our age.

Preachers often express the difficulty of so framing their sermons that they speak to a wide variety of people and needs in the congregation. But the same sort of consideration applies to the prayers. Spoken prayers can enable people to pray, or can drive them very far from prayer. Some prayers can be so specific as to border on the trivial, and others so general as to seem related to nothing. This is a highly sensitive area and requires the most careful preparation. In his book on preaching, Colin Morris confesses that he has often paid too little attention to the prayers which he is to lead.[8] 'Conceiving' prayer or even composing biddings requires at least time set aside for the purpose.

Four kinds of prayer

1. Praise

Adoration or praise is usually broadcast over the whole act of Christian worship, and is certainly not confined to those parts of it specifically designed for prayer. Praise of God is expressed through many of the psalms, through such ancient songs of the Church as the Te Deum, the Gloria in Excelsis and the Sanctus, and through the centuries of Christian hymnody. But sometimes in worship there are specific acts of adoration. The Book of Common Order provides such; and a Presbyterian contributor to *Getting the Liturgy Right* has set out some problems in devising this kind of prayer:

> Much of the material inherited is suggestive of the throne room of a mediaeval monarch or of an ancient middle-eastern potentate – models remote from the experience of modern man (even with the benefit of TV reconstructions). If the power and love of God may be selected as two key concepts for the evoking of adoration it is important that we do not speak of power in a manner which is cold or impersonal (which could easily be the case if we think of that power simply in terms of the awe-inspiring immensities of the created order opened up by scientific research) nor speak of love in terms which make it anything less than awe-inspiring in its scope and depth. For this purpose we need a language which is rich and paradoxical.[9]

All this is difficult to achieve, but the attempt must be

made. We must not underestimate the power of the basic facts of the gospel to evoke faith and enable praise. Although much modern hymnody has sought to fill gaps in our heritage from the past, there are still those who want to write new songs about Christ's birth and death and resurrection – despite the existence of excellent material on such themes. And despite psalms which proclaim the glory of God (and notable paraphrases of them like those of Isaac Watts), we can still have such verses as these:

> Lord of the boundless curves of space
> And time's deep mystery,
> To your creative might we trace
> All nature's energy.
>
> Your Spirit gave the living cell
> Its hidden, vital force:
> The instincts which all life impel
> Derive from you, their source.
>
> Yours is the image stamped on man,
> Though marred by man's own sin;
> And yours the liberating plan
> Again his soul to win. [10]

These three stanzas from the very sure pen of Albert Bayly reveal the need both for such writing and for such themes in our worship.

2. Penitence

Prayers of penitence need to steer between the extremes of overstatement and understatement. Post-Reformation worship certainly suffered from overstatement; it was dominated by a sense of sin, emphasized partly by the theology of the age, and partly by the removal of the confessional. But equally we must not be tempted to minimize the reality of evil or the responsibility of the individual. Our forms of confession must not simply dwell on what we have done or left undone, but on the fact that we have missed the way, failed to reach the mark. And they must be corporate as well as individual. We are what we are partly because the Church and the world are what they are; but we also contribute to the present state of the Church and the world.

Alongside real expressions of penitence must be no less real affirmations of God's pardoning love and renewing grace. Our expression of sin must be strong enough to help us see our need for forgiveness and to appreciate something of its cost; but guilt and lamentation must not be so loud as to let us think that no such forgiveness is possible.

A book of satirical prayers published a few years ago[11] points out the danger of the two extremes to which we have referred. Probably prayers of this kind have to be rewritten for each generation. Biblical material can help, particularly (if rightly understood) Psalm 51. There is a place (Ash Wednesday is traditional) for extended forms of self-examination and confession. The Commination Service of the Prayer Book did this in a very drastic way. A vast improvement upon it was the little-known 'exhortation' printed in an appendix to the book proposed in 1928. More recent are the penitential rites now used corporately in many Roman Catholic churches.

3. *Thanksgiving*

Thanksgiving has long been the Cinderella of Anglican worship, despite the fact that it is to the Anglican tradition that the whole Church owes one of the finest and most enduring of prayers – usually called the General Thanksgiving. It is obviously impossible to draw too sharp a distinction between praise and thanksgiving; praise or adoration is often understood as our response to the nature of God as disclosed in his dealing with his world, and thanksgiving as response to particular experiences of his nature which are ours.

The rubric in Rite A of the ASB says, under the general title of 'The Intercession', 'intercessions and thanksgivings are led by the President or by others'. In his valuable practical commentary on Series 3[12] Michael Perham warned us against incorporating into this part of worship that which properly belongs to the eucharistic prayer itself. Similar criticism has been made of the first post-communion prayer in the same rite. But where intercession is made, there is surely room for a corresponding act of thanksgiving. For example prayers for the sick could be accompanied by thanksgiving not only for those who have recovered, but for the gift of health and for the many agents of healing in our world. At other services it is important to recall the things for which we should be grateful as those which we need. Thanksgiving is always good for the soul; at times it may seem the only possible kind of prayer.

4. Petition

Petition falls into two parts – for ourselves, and for other people (when it is more often called intercession). But the two are closely linked, because we are part of the world for which we pray, and, as we have often been reminded in recent years, we cannot love our neighbour as ourselves if we do not love ourselves.

All kinds of pitfall seem to surround the practical conduct of such prayers. The freer form of Anglican intercession means that people often seem uncertain as to whether they are addressing God or their fellow worshippers e.g.

Almighty God our heavenly Father, you promised through your Son Jesus Christ to hear us when we pray in faith: Let us pray for the Church in this place. . . .

59

which suggests that God is being invited to join in prayer himself! Again such prayers can be so long and detailed that they sound like the list made out for the cash-and-carry. It was in the early centuries that Augustine wrote:

> God does not ask us to tell him about our needs in order to learn about them, but in order that we may be capable of receiving his gifts. [13]

Yet again the prayer must not sound so general as to be applicable to nothing in particular.

But, above all, we must avoid what have been called 'horizontal prayers'. They must not make points or get at someone in the congregation. They must not assume a political stance or ecclesiastical opinion or even an historical judgement that is open to question and may not be shared by all present. This is particularly likely to happen in the small group or prayer-meeting but it can occur in larger gatherings as well. Whether one could say 'Amen' to a certain prayer offered not long ago in one of our cathedrals depended on which side one would have found oneself in the Civil War!

Non-verbal prayer

Not even public prayer is entirely a matter of words. Many churches – perhaps not enough – are experimenting with the periods of silence suggested in many of our modern liturgies. These can give such valuable breathing space in worship – enabling the individual to contribute his or her own intercession or aspiration to the common worship. The value of silence depends on two things; first, that people are helped in their understanding of how to use it, and secondly, that they know roughly how long it will last.

There is also a place for symbolism in prayer. The

lighted candle has long been a symbol of individual prayer in some parts of the Christian Church. If portable candles are used in worship, they could be taken to the place at which the prayers are offered as well as to that in which the Gospel is read. The use of incense has long marked a dividing-point in Anglican churchmanship, but it is a form of Christian symbolism to which fresh thought could be given. Since it is often in the Bible a symbol of prayer, it could be used perhaps during prayer or meditation rather than as a fussy accompaniment to a lot of other activity.

'Let us pray' does not mean that everyone will do so; many will be enabled or disabled to do by what is said and done after that exhortation.

Notes

1. Donald Coggan, *The Prayers of the New Testament* (Hodder & Stoughton original), Mowbray, 1984.
2. William W. Simpson, *Jewish Prayer and Worship*, SCM, 1965.
3. G. A. Studdert Kennedy, *The Unutterable Beauty* (Hodder & Stoughton original), Mowbray, 1983.
4. Howard Spring, *Fame is the Spur*, Collins, 1940, p.37.
5. Quoted by J. G. Huxtable in *The Renewal of Worship*, ed. Jasper, OUP, 1965, p.58.
6. ed. Jasper, op. cit. p.61.
7. BBC, *New Every Morning*, 1973, BBC, p.viii.
8. Colin Morris, *The Word and the Words*, Ch. 6, Epworth 1975.
9. J. C. Stewart, in *Getting the Liturgy Right*, ed. Jasper, SPCK, 1982, p.39.
10. *More Hymns for Today*, 160, Clowes, 1980.
11. David Head, *He Sent Leanness*, Epworth, 1959.
12. Michael Perham, *The Eucharist*, Alcuin/SPCK, 1978, p.55.
13. Quoted in *Liturgy Reshaped*, ed. Stephenson, SPCK, 1982, p.33.

6. THE GOD WHO MEETS US

Sacraments

When Pope John Paul II was making his plans to visit this island, it was announced that his theme would be 'The Seven Sacraments'. There were some whose immediate reaction was one of regret that he should choose a theme more likely to underline divisions than to remove them. In the event, however, it made little difference to the ecumenical impact of the visit.

Traditional Roman Catholic theology has recognized seven sacraments – Baptism, the Eucharist, Confirmation, Marriage, Ordination, Penance and Unction. The Anglican articles of religion said that the last five

> are not to be counted for sacraments of the Gospel, being such as have grown partly of the corrupt following of the Apostles, partly are states of life allowed in the Scriptures; but yet have not like nature of Sacraments with Baptism, and the Lord's Supper, for that they have not any visible sign or ceremony ordained of God. (Article 25)

But for a long time many Anglicans have rejected the categorical distinction of the Articles. Some have wanted to use the word 'sacramental' much more widely, whilst according particular honour to Baptism and the Lord's Supper, whilst others have openly referred to Penance and Confirmation as sacraments. At the other end of the Christian spectrum, bodies like the Society of Friends and the Salvation Army have rejected the sacraments as such – sometimes as a reaction against anything mechanical, sometimes because they have believed that these things are to be understood in terms of spiritual experience, and sometimes because they have wanted to stress that the whole of life is sacramental. In recent years more radical critics of the New Testament have questioned the old certainty that it was appropriate to speak of Baptism and the Eucharist as sacraments because they were clearly instituted by Christ Himself. [1]

But in the mainstream churches, Baptism and the Eucharist are regarded as sacraments of the gospel, and to these we shall give most attention in this chapter. Before doing so, it may be useful to say rather more about sacraments in general. The well known definition of the Prayer Book Catechism still seems to stand the test of time – namely that a sacrament is 'an outward and visible sign of an inward and spiritual grace'. Throughout the Old Testament, we find examples of objects which God is seen to use as signs of his presence – like the ark of the covenant and the temple itself. Moreover, we find throughout the Old Testament that which a former generation described as 'the scandal of the particular'. God chooses a particular people and so trains them that prophets come to realize that through this people, his light will be carried out into the whole world. He appoints a particular day to be kept holy in order that all days shall be recognized as his. He uses matter and he uses time. Through these 'particulars' he meets his people. Often, they miss the point of it all, and suppose that provided they attend to the particular, the general does not matter. So we get the prophets' denunciation of sacrifice that does not result in righteousness, and Jesus' own condemnation of those who so misunderstood the Sabbath as to suppose that works of healing and compassion were forbidden on that day. But the misuse of such ordinances does not always mean that they should be abolished. God continues to use matter and time. The early Christians began to regard the resurrection day as the Lord's day, and to believe that they were responding to his will when they used water, bread and wine as the means and signs of his grace. The great twentieth century theologian, Paul Tillich, believed that the more we were estranged from nature, the less we were able to appreciate the character of sacraments:

> For in the sacraments, nature participates in the process of salvation. Bread and wine, water and light and all the great elements of nature become the bearers of spiritual meaning and saving power. [2]

Goethe was not alone in believing 'the highest cannot be spoken; it can only be acted' and Augustine described Baptism and the Eucharist as 'visible words'. [3]

Baptism

For many years scholars have questioned whether we can demonstrate that Jesus himself told his disciples to baptize their converts. The references are at the end of the gospels of St Mark and St Matthew. In the case of St Mark, this is one of the several possible 'endings' to the book, since, so far as we can tell, the most ancient versions end abruptly with the resurrection. In St Matthew (28) the final verses are

> 'Go forth and make all nations my disciples; baptize men everywhere in the name of the Father and the Son and the Holy Spirit, and teach them to observe all that I have commanded you. And be assured, I am with you always, to the end of time.'

Now this sounds more like a description of the practice of the Church when St Matthew's gospel assumed its final form than a precise account of Ascension Day. Nowhere else in Jesus' teaching do we find specific Trinitarian reference, and the accounts of Baptism in the Acts of the Apostles suggest that it was 'in the name of Jesus'.

But Jesus was himself baptized, and all the gospel narratives record the incident in some detail. It is interesting to note *en passant* that the incident, always regarded as of great importance in the East, has, until recently, received scant liturgical recognition in the West. It is now a Sunday 'theme' in The Alternative Service Book. It is possible that the disciples took Jesus' baptism as reason enough to baptize, and likely also that Jesus emphasized it – though not in the developed form of St Matthew.

Both Baptism and the Eucharist played a considerable part in the actual shaping of the New Testament. Various passages have been claimed as referring to Baptism. This has been seen, for example as the background to the first letter of Peter; and the letter to the Ephesians contains what may be a fragment of an early baptismal hymn (5.14). Most explicit of all are the verses from Romans 6 which run

> By baptism we were buried with him, and lay dead, in order that, as Christ was raised from the dead in the splendour of the Father, so also we might set our feet upon the new path of life.

The practice of Baptism seems to have passed through four main stages. In the first, it looks as though it was administered almost spontaneously and on demand. In Acts 2 we have an account of Peter's sermon at Pentecost. In reply to the question 'What are we to do?' Peter replies 'Repent and be baptized, every one of you, in the name of Jesus the Messiah for the forgiveness of your sins.' The chapter goes on to record that some three thousand were added to the number of the Christians on that day. When allowance is made for exaggeration and possible telescoping of the story, it does seem that the only preparation

65

required for Baptism was repentance – a turning from sin to Christ, and a profession of faith in him. The accounts of the Ethiopian eunuch (ch. 8) and the gaoler at Philippi (ch. 16) are particular examples of this instant Baptism.

In the second stage, Baptism became an occasion for which a fairly long and arduous preparation was made. Sometimes the change in policy is ascribed to persecution; certainly it arose from a fear that people might be baptized without properly understanding its significance and its demands. E. C. Whitaker[4] speaks of 350 – 450 as the century in which the rites of adult Baptism reached their full flowering. So through the season of Lent there would be the exorcisms, the scrutinies, the fastings, the creed delivered secretly in order that it might be learned by the candidates who were to be baptized on Easter Eve.

It is impossible to determine precisely when children were admitted to these rites. Much ink has been used in the debate about whether or not infant Baptism is suggested in the New Testament. Certainly there is no specific suggestion that it was: and the very young could not fulfil even the very simple requirement for Baptism described there. But there are references to households being baptized; and some who appreciate the solidarity of the Jewish family find it hard to believe that children would be excluded. The debate is likely to continue – pending fresh evidence.

But the third stage is emphatically one that includes children. When Christianity became not only a licit religion, but virtually the established faith of the Roman Empire, Baptism began to be administered at birth, and adult Baptism grew rare. This stage is illustrated by the rubrics of the Book of Common Prayer:

The Curates of every Parish shall often admonish the people, that they defer not the Baptism of their Children longer than the first or second Sunday after their birth, . . . unless upon a great and reasonable cause, to be approved by the Curate.

and later with relation to catechism:

And all Fathers, Mothers, Masters and Dames shall cause their Children, Servants and Prentices (which have not learned their Catechism) to come to the Church at the time appointed, and obediently to hear, and be ordered by the Curate. . . .

Thus the full process of Christian initiation became the normal consequence of living in a society where the boundaries of Church and State seemed coterminous.

The fourth stage is our own. Sometimes this is described as the post-Christian age; it is certainly post-Constantinian in outlook. It is marked by an increasing refusal to administer baptism on demand; it is marked also by a decreasing demand for baptism. Within the Churches are many who believe that in our present circumstances, Baptism should not be administered to infants at all – which must delight the Baptists who have thought so for four hundred years! More common is the view that Baptism should be restricted to the children of practising members of the Church (not always easy to define) and that it can be justified only if there is a reasonable guarantee that children will be brought up in the fellowship of the Church and within earshot of its instruction. Very widely held is the belief that Baptism is always the *concern* of the local church and should therefore be administered in the course of public worship rather than as some private family affair.

Liturgical revision has been in the context of theological and pastoral questions about Christian initiation that continue to be debated. What has emerged in contemporary service-books is twofold; first, there is full provision for the Baptism of adults or believers; and secondly, rubrics are so designed as to indicate that the normal occasion for any kind of Baptism is when the congregation is at worship. Thus in The Alternative Service Book adult Baptism and Confirmation are seen as the norm from which infant Baptism is derived – a reversal of the arrangements in the Prayer Book. Moreover the rubrics of the book are so framed that Baptism can be incorporated into the normal Sunday service without undue prolongation of that service. In short, everything is done to encourage and facilitate the administration of Baptism in this way. The weaning away of people from 'private' Baptism is largely an Anglican problem, and it is rather surprising that it should be so. For the 1662 Prayer Book had set out two reasons why Baptism should be public – so that the congregation should witness the Baptism and presumably welcome the baptized, and in order that all present should remember the implications of their own baptism.

The first is, as we have seen, being increasingly recognized. In the ASB, the congregation has more than one vocal part of which the most significant is:

> We welcome you into the Lord's Family,
> We are members together of the body of Christ;
> We are children of the same heavenly Father;
> We are inheritors together of the kingdom of God.
> We welcome you.

But the second is no less important. So it is that the ASB provides also a service called 'The Renewal of Baptismal Vows on Various Occasions'. In this service the congregation reaffirms both the three-fold decision and the three-fold profession of faith that is made both at Baptism and Confirmation. This service is recommended for use at Easter in accordance with ancient usage and increasing modern practice.[5] The New Year is also suggested – where it would correspond in some way with the Methodist Covenant Service, generally held at that time.

'Other suitable occasions' are also mentioned, and could include a mission or particular parish enterprise. It should not be 'sprung' upon a congregation, and they should have time to prepare for it. It could become too familiar and easy. It is sometimes used at the enthronement of a bishop or the installation of a priest – with the result that the service becomes one long interrogation.

The Eucharist

Probably the most important achievement of the twentieth century liturgical movement has been the restoration of Baptism and the Eucharist to that centrality which they seem to have held in the very first centuries of the Christian Church. We turn now to the place of the Eucharist in the New Testament.

The occasion on which the Lord's Supper was held has been another much-debated question of New Testament scholarship. The synoptic gospels tell us that Jesus 'did this' at the Passover meal. The chronology of the fourth gospel is different, putting the Supper before the Passover and posing the question 'What was the occasion?' But St John does not mention the institution of the Eucharist, and instead records the feet-washing; yet at least one chapter (6) of the gospel is generally seen as a profound meditation on the meaning of the Eucharist. Another subject of critical scholarship is provided by the varied accounts of the institution narrative – Mark, Matthew, Luke, and Paul in the first letter to the Corinthians. In that same letter and in the Acts of the Apostles we have references to the breaking of the bread as well as fuller accounts of the meeting for worship.

By the time we reach Justin Martyr, to whom reference has been made in earlier chapters, the Eucharist is celebrated on a Sunday, and, after readings, sermon, prayers and the Peace, 'bread is brought and wine and water' and 'the President offers up prayers and thanksgivings to the best of his ability'. We know very little about the content of those prayers and thanksgivings until a century later, when Hippolytus provides us with the first extant eucharistic prayer. The dominant notes are thanksgiving and hope for the fulfilment of God's kingdom, and the prayer has served as a model, both in its general framework and some of its language, for those used in our present day Eucharists.[6]

So we pass to the years of elaboration and enrichment – as well as those of sophistication and clericalization. Some of the changes that came about reflected the ideas of their day, and some were necessitated by circumstances. Some brought undoubted richness to the service, some emphasized one part of it to the exclusion of others. By the time of the Reformation, the general effect was a distancing of the people from eucharistic action, so that the laity became passive spectators – very seldom receiving Holy Communion themselves. There followed the bitter controversies of the Reformation, centring around the nature of the eucharistic sacrifices and the meaning of the presence of Christ in the sacrament. The eucharistic prayer in the reformed Churches tended to be limited to a rehearsal by word and action of what happened in the Upper Room. We noted earlier Karl Barth's comment about the Catholic sacrament without word, and the Protestant word without sacrament (ch. 4).

So finally we come to the remarkable achievements of our own century and to happenings which belong to the lifetime of many of our present worshippers. Through both the ecumenical and liturgical movements, there has been a common desire to go back to origins and to shape things afresh. This has resulted:

1. in a recovery of the Eucharist as the normative act of worship on Sundays in the majority of Christian traditions;
2. in a general recognition of the twin importance of word

and sacrament, the one being seen as complementary to the other;

3. in movement towards a common, clear and coherent shape to the service itself – especially in the eucharistic action itself where taking, giving thanks, breaking the bread and distributing the elements are all given special significance;

4. in substantial agreement about the broad contents of the eucharistic prayer, and a new recognition that it may be diversely expressed (e.g. the four prayers in Rite A of the ASB);

5. in the development of ways by which it becomes clear that the Eucharist is the action of all present – with increased participation by the laity, and the central table or altar generally recognized as ideal, even when, for practical reasons, it cannot be achieved.

In consequence of all this, the contemporary rites of the Church of England, the Roman Catholic Church, the Methodist Church, the United Reformed Church and the Church of Scotland are more remarkable for their similarities, certainly in structure and often in language, than for their differences. Moreover the last decade has seen Anglicans and Roman Catholics sitting down to hammer out apparently irreconcilable views of real presence and eucharistic sacrifice and finding that although differences might remain, they had in the past been exaggerated by ignorance, prejudice and misunderstanding.

It would be possible for all this to end in self-congratulation and complacency. We could suppose that now we had 'arrived' and we could boast that we were wiser than our fathers. But there is still much to be achieved. The Eucharist which Christ believed would be a sign of unity is still a sign of disunity. The fact that the Roman Catholic Church does not normally receive at its altars Christians of other Churches can be a source of pain and frustration to ecumenical groups and most certainly so to partners in mixed marriages. The failure of the proposals for covenant in this country still makes communion together only an occasional event. And the fact that the Churches which are growing most rapidly today are very different in ethos from the Churches of the West means that eventually new forms of reconciliation and new ways of integration may have to be sought.

And there is also much to learn. Well-devised forms of the Eucharist do not mean that we have 'arrived'. It is possible for the new Anglican services to be misused, for example, by including too many of the options; or by allowing one part of the service to be habitually out of proportion to the rest; or by perpetuating ceremonies that obscure the meaning of the rite; or by failing to develop ceremonies that would clarify that meaning. A few such dangers are mentioned at the end of Richard Buxton's contribution to *Liturgy Reshaped;*[7] but many essayists there warn us against over-confidence about what is primitive (and therefore worthy of inclusion now) and the whole book suggests that the process of liturgical revision must be ongoing.

We are not likely to reach a stage where either in our thinking or in our practice we have exhausted all the meaning of the Eucharist, nor one in which we do not need to be learning truths about it that we have forgotten or never known. Dom Gregory Dix' *The Shape of the Liturgy* has long been a familiar volume even in a small private theological library. It remains a great book, even though it is not quite the 'bible' that liturgical students once supposed it to be. But in a much-quoted passage he asks of 'do this',

Was ever another commandment so obeyed? Men have found no better thing to do for kings at their crowning and for criminals going to the scaffold; for armies in triumph or a bride and bridegroom in a country church; for the wisdom of a Parliament, or a sick old woman afraid to die. [8]

Dix' own enumeration of the occasions of its celebration, reminds us again of the manifold meaning of the Eucharist.

Symbols

Fresh thinking about the sacraments has brought about a new evaluation of the symbols inherent in them, as well as of those that surround them, and amongst the writings on this subject we may note two essays – one by a Roman Catholic and one by an Anglican.[9] The symbol of the table and the meal has been important not only for appreciation of the Eucharist, but for the *agape* in which it was originally set. This is expressed sometimes in the coffee party which follows the Parish Communion, or in more particular ways like the love-feast of the early Methodists which has, in recent years, sometimes been used where full sacramental fellowship may not be expressed. The symbol of light still remains powerful; and the candle which is used for a party becomes naturally the lighted candle at Baptism. Candle-lit services associated both with Christmas and Easter are much more than an expression of sentimentality or nostalgia, but a return to what is clemental.

Another writer has warned us against the emasculation of symbols:

> The reason for this probably lies in the fact that scriptural symbols are rather messy or inconvenient. Fire, water, oil, ashes – to name but a few – can soon make an awful mess, and it is not surprising, therefore, that before long Christian sacristans began to look around for tame, nice, clean, ecclesiastical varieties of these rather improper and inconvenient symbols.[10]

From here we get to the 'wafer' that does not remotely resemble bread, and to the specially-made ecclesiastical wine. Alongside this danger are two others: the perpetuation of 'symbols' which have lost their power to symbolize anything, and the failure to look for new symbols that do speak to our generation.

It is through symbols that we move somewhat nearer to the Quaker insistence, noted at the beginning of this chapter, that all life is meant to be sacramental, that everything we encounter can be a sign of God's grace. This is indeed the goal of those Christians who do believe in the sacraments. It is God who meets us here, and we go to meet him here in order that we may know him everywhere.

Notes

1. A useful popular discussion may be found in Gerald Priestland's *Priestland's Progress*.
2. Paul Tillich, *The Shaking of the Foundations*, Pelican, 1962, p.91.
3. Quoted in J. S. Whale, *Christian Doctrine*, CUP, 1952, pp.155 – 7.
4. E. C. Whitaker, *The Baptismal Liturgy*, SPCK, 1981.
5. See for example, the Joint Liturgical Group's publication, *Holy Week Services*, SPCK, 1983.
6. A text for students, edited by Geoffrey Cuming, is available in Grove Liturgical Studies.
7. Ed. Stevenson, *Liturgy Reshaped*, SPCK, 1982.
8. G. Dix, *The Shape of the Liturgy*, Dacre Press, 1945, p.744.
9. Balthasar Fischer in *Liturgy Reshaped*, SPCK, 1982; and Hugh Montefiore in *Thinking about the Eucharist*, SCM, 1972.
10. Michael Marshall, *Renewal in Worship*, Marshall, Morgan & Scott, 1982, p.96.

7. THE GOD WHO RECEIVES US

The God who listens to us and the God who meets us is also one who delights in the worship which his people offer him. In parts of the Old Testament, this is expressed through sacrifice; in other parts, greater stress is laid on the offering of the hearts and minds and wills of human beings. The contention of the first chapter was that if God does indeed correspond to the biblical witness to him, then worship must be the inevitable response to him. Belief and worship go together.

But does God want worship – does he enjoy praise? In an earlier chapter, we recalled Howard Spring's character, Birley Artingstall who, after he had made his regular and very stylized contribution to the prayer meeting was always pathetically anxious for recognition. Now obviously God is not modelled upon his frail creatures. But if our capacity for love derives from God, then the human situation must in some way reflect him; and love, as we know, is both giving and receiving. But God seeks our praise because that praise indicates that our hearts and minds are set on him in whom alone we find our fulfilment and our destiny. Moreover, in the Bible, the distinction so often drawn is not so much between belief and unbelief, as between right belief and wrong belief – not so much between worship and the lack of it as between true and false worship. When the Psalmist wrote, 'The fool hath said in his heart "There is no God",' he is probably not thinking of an atheist but of those who live as if God did not exist – giving him neither the praise of their lips nor that of their lives.

Our offering

Our offering of praise is essentially response to God as he is revealed to us. In the first chapter of his book *The Paradox of Worship*, Michael Perry outlines the disadvantages of the common equation of worship with 'worthship'.[1] He suggests that this can easily decline into a man-centred activity. When people say 'only the best will do for worship' they are in danger of supposing that the best will do. When great music is described as 'an offering of worship', it may or may not be such. It becomes Christian worship when it is seen as response to God who is the source of love as well as beauty, of truth as well as righteousness.

In the letter to the Ephesians, (5.19; Col. 3.16), Christians are exhorted to 'speak to one another in psalms and hymns and songs, singing and making music in their hearts to the Lord'. Singing has remained a constant and normal physical way of expressing praise, and for this reason will occupy most of this chapter, though, at the end, we shall try to show that it is not the only way in which praise can be offered.

Psalms

The Psalms do in fact, perfectly illustrate the main point we have been making about Christian worship. They are centred on God — who is always there, even when the Psalmist is dissatisfied with him, and would like to get away from him. But when, in Psalm 98, trumpets, horns and harps are summoned to praise, that praise is directed to the God 'who has done marvellous things'. Psalm 150 ends 'let everything that hath breath praise the Lord', and this praise, again, is not directed to a vague 'first cause' but to the God who has been revealed as Yahweh. The Psalms come from a variety of dates and circumstances in Israel's history, but they were to become the praise-book of her Temple. Doubtless they were also part of individual devotion, and it is significant that of the 'seven words' ascribed to Jesus on his cross, three are from the Psalter.

From the beginning, Psalms seem to have been part of Christian worship, and they were eventually to form a major element in the services and offices of the Church. But their use has extended beyond formal worship, and a valuable book still to be found on the shelves of second-hand booksellers reveals something of what they have meant to individuals and communities belonging to or affected by the Christian tradition. [2]

The Psalms are always being rediscovered. This happened at the Reformation. Just prior to that, they were probably not widely known amongst the laity. Parts of them were used in the Mass as well as in the offices, but they were in Latin. Reformation service-books lean heavily on the Psalms as acts of praise. In the second English Prayer Book of 1552, Cranmer offered Psalms as alternatives to the Benedictus, Magnificat and Nunc Dimittis. This is often interpreted as Protestant prejudice against the use of canticles which had been part of the medieval services, but it could well represent Protestant enthusiasm for the rediscovered Psalter. More important in this period and more widely used were the various metrical versions – designed to popularize and facilitate the singing of the Psalms.

Perhaps we are waiting for another such rediscovery on a large scale. The Psalms are probably not well known at present except by habitués of cathedral-type services. In Anglicanism, the decline of Matins and Evensong as popular Sunday services has meant a decline in psalmody, and although both forms of the ASB Eucharist recommend the use of a psalm between the Old and New Testament readings, this is not mandatory, and is frequently ignored.

For the last hundred years or so, the announcement of

a psalm to an Anglican congregation has suggested a difficult operation. Most people held in their hands the unpointed version of the Psalms to be found in the Prayer Book. From a distant corner of the church came the playing of a chant, often pitched fairly high. The congregation was expected to fit the words they read to the tune they heard. If there were a choir, they trailed behind its lead as best they could, but often found that this was the weakest part of the choir's repertoire. If there were no choir the situation resembled the days when there was no judge in Israel, and 'every man did what was right in his own eyes'. The strong-minded and the strong-voiced then set the pace, and such leaders were not necessarily the most melodious members of the assembly.

It is therefore not surprising that the Psalms have tended to lose popularity. But there are in fact a number of ways in which they may be used. The ASB provided for the Psalms a pointing which is simple and whose principles can be quite quickly learned. If the choir is good, the Psalms can be seen as a form of meditation − the congregation sitting, reading and listening to what is sung. The Grail and other modern Roman versions suggest a method involving perhaps cantor and choir, with the congregation singing an antiphon or refrain. And there are the various attempts to put the Psalms in metre − dating in Anglicanism from the days when the Old Version of Sternhold and Hopkins or the New Version of Tate and Brady were often bound up with the Prayer Book itself.

Metrical versions are not necessarily bad. Anglicans are sometimes scornful of Scottish metrical psalms, and it has to be confessed that if the Scottish Psalter of 1929 is put alongside Coverdale's translation in the Prayer Book, the latter will take the literary honours. But there are the versions of Isaac Watts − some of very high quality; in the writer's opinion 'Our God our help in ages past' (with the possessive opening pronoun restored) is as fine a translation of Psalm 90 as any. Erik Routley's 'New songs of celebration render' brings out features of Psalm 98 often unnoticed, and George Herbert's, 'The God of love my shepherd is', is generally agreed to be an exquisite rendering of Psalm 23. A book called *Psalm Praise*[3] is used in some churches; it has prose passages set to chants, but many more in metre. Although useful, its limited group of contributors makes it a little monochrome. A book of this kind, ecumenically devised and containing a variety of translations and ways of using the Psalms could be of great value to all the Churches.

The Psalms are much too good to lose, and congregations need to explore new ways of recovering them for worship. Although many of them cry out to be sung, their recitation either corporately or antiphonally remains a possibility that ought not to be ignored – especially in small congregations.

We have spoken of the Psalms in general. Some of them immediately seem admirable vehicles of Christian devotion. But what of the rest? Should they all be used? Most churches adopt some principle of selectivity; but the Roman Catholic and Anglican churches use the whole psalter, and until recently, Anglican clergy were expected to recite it right through every month. The Psalms in the ASB lectionary are spread over a longer period, and portions of them are bracketed. But much that remains is sub-Christian, and some of it is vindictive and self-righteous. Many people have defended the 'cursing' psalms – C. S. Lewis being one such writer.[4] They have pointed out that the Psalms witness to the reality of evil, and that this is important in an age which sees good and bad in relative terms. Others have pointed out that the psalmists' reflection of every kind of human emotion is good and healthy; even if we pretend to be pious in the presence of God, he knows very well when we are not. Such arguments are weighty, but not altogether convincing when they are used to defend the practice of a dogged recitation of the whole Psalter; and it is curious that some people approach the Psalms with a fundamentalism that they would not think of applying to other books of the Old Testament.

This leads us to a wider question: can the Psalms be rearranged, even sometimes rewritten as *Christian* praises? One person who thought they could was Isaac Watts, who produced in 1718 *The Psalms of David imitated in the Language of the New Testament and applied to the Christian State and Worship*. In his original and pungent preface, he asked his readers:

> Have you not felt a new Joy spring within you, when you could speak your own Desires and Hopes, your own Faith, Love and Zeal in the Language of the holy Psalmist? Have not your Spirits taken Wing and mounted up near to God and Glory, with the Song of David on your tongue? But on a sudden the Clerk has proposed the next Line to your Lips with dark Sayings and Prophecies, with Burnt-offerings or Hyssop, with New-moons and Trumpets and Timbrels in it, with Confessions of sins which you never committed, with Complaints of Sorrows which you never felt; cursing such Enemies as you never had, giving Thanks for such Victories as you never obtained, or leading you to speak in your own Persons of Things, Places and Actions that you never knew. And how have all your Souls been discomposed at once, and the Strings of harmony all untuned.

Watts goes on to explain his own policy:

> Where the Psalmist describes Religion by the Fear of God, I have often joined Faith and Love to it. . . . Where he talks of sacrificing Goats or Bullocks, I rather choose to mention the Sacrifice of Christ, the Lamb of God. Where he attends the Ark with

shouting into Zion, I sing the Ascension of my
Saviour into Heaven or his Presence in his Church
on Earth. [5]

Watts said he would always have David speak the
common sense of a Christian, and it has been pointed out
that he often made David speak like an eighteenth
century Englishman whose sympathies were Whig! But
much of his work has survived in its own right – even
though few who sing his fine hymn 'Jesus shall reign'
realize that it is Psalm 72 Christianized. Yet Watts raised
questions which have not been completely answered, and
his preface raises them again when, in a cathedral Evensong, Psalms 84 and 85 are preceded by 83.

There is a place for new versions – new paraphases,
even – of the Psalms alongside those which are more
literal renderings of the text. The Christian use of the
Psalter is two-fold. In them we witness to the continuity
of what God has done in both Old and New Testaments;
but we also witness to the essential newness of what God
has done in Christ. It is surely likely that when the first
Christians sang the Psalms, the ancient texts took on a
new meaning. 'O sing unto the Lord a new song' said the
psalmist, and it will be a 'new song' for those who believe
that God is always doing new things.

Hymns

The psalmists' injunction to 'Sing a new song to the Lord'
seems to have been taken seriously by the early Church.
Scattered throughout the New Testament are what seem
to be the texts of early Christian hymns or parts of them.
We noted in the last chapter what may be a fragment of a
baptismal hymn in the letter to the Ephesians. The ASB
contains a number of alternative canticles from the letter
to the Philippians and the book of Revelation which may

well be early Christian hymns. The Sanctus, Gloria in Excelsis and Te Deum belong also to fairly early hymnody. Hymns grew in use through the monastic offices, but they were sung devotionally and in great processions.

But hymn-singing as we now know it in the churches of the West stems from the Reformation − from the chorales of Germany and the psalms and paraphrases of the Swiss Reformation. It took its greatest surge forward with the Evangelical revival of the eighteenth century − with Watts and Doddridge the Dissenters, Newton and Cowper the Anglicans, and with the Wesleys and their new movement. From that time forward, it became the part of public worship in which the congregation most readily participated, and sometimes the one which it found most memorable. People often learn and remember their religion by the hymns they sing. The Wesleys intended this to happen and were therefore deeply concerned about the doctrinal content of the hymns. In his preface to the 1780 collection, John Wesley wrote:

> (the book is) large enough to contain all the important truths of our holy religion, whether speculative or practical; yea, to illustrate them all and to prove them, both by Scripture and reason; and this is done in a regular order. The hymns are not carelessly jumbled together, but carefully ranged under proper heads according to the experience of real Christians, so that this book is, in effect, a little body of experimental and practical divinity. [6]

Since the eighteenth century, there have been further explosions of hymnody. One was in the nineteenth century and a consequence of the Oxford Movement − when many ancient Greek and Latin hymns were translated and brought into use. The last quarter of a century has similarly been a great period for the writing of hymns and, to a lesser extent, of tunes. In the main, this hymn-writing has sought to fulfil some obvious gaps in our standard collections. It has, for example, produced hymns on the social aspects of the Christian faith, and sought to deal realistically with such occasions as Harvest Thanksgiving. At the same time it has tried to meet new liturgical needs – among them, the growing centrality of the Eucharist and the placing of Baptism in the context of public worship on Sundays. Until recently, few hymn-books contained appropriate material for the Sunday when the baptism of Jesus forms the theme. And there are those who have written on subjects for which there is already plentiful material – simply because they have felt constrained to 'sing a new song to the Lord'. In consequence most of the standard hymn-books produced in the fifties now have a supplement. We are only just beginning to move from the era of the supplements into that of new standard collections.

The plethora of material underlines the need of discrimination. What principles should govern our use of hymns? In the first place, no hymn should be chosen carelessly; 'when in doubt sing a hymn' cannot be a good liturgical axiom. The present writer does not subscribe to the doctrine held by many of his fellow Anglicans that hymns ought to be used to cover up any movement or activity in worship. If the movement is important (e.g. entry of the bride) or symbolic (e.g. presentation of the elements) surely it ought to be allowed to speak for itself and not be smothered by singing. At the same time, the proper and reverent singing of a hymn requires the full attention of those taking part in it.

This general point of underlining the *importance* of hymn-singing suggests four more:
1. The hymn must faithfully reflect the truths of Christianity. The most enduring hymns are those which

are biblical in basis, and this accounts for the continued popularity of Wesley and Watts, and makes them seem nearer to our own generation than (say) some missionary hymns of the nineteenth century. This does not mean that all hymns ought to be four-square and literal – Wesley, after all, seldom wrote direct paraphrases and more often his verses contain a whole kaleidoscope of texts. Certainly, there is room for the poetic and the allusive, as in this modern translation:

> There in God's garden stands the tree of wisdom
> whose leaves hold forth the healing of the nations:
> tree of all knowledge, tree of all compassion,
> tree of all beauty.
>
> Its name is Jesus, name that says 'our Saviour'
> there on its branches see the scars of suffering:
> see where the tendrils of our human selfhood
> feed on its life-blood. [7]

On the other hand, when we look at the moderately popular 'I vow to thee my country' with this criterion in mind, we may question whether either its sentiments or its language make it a Christian hymn – despite the excellent intentions of its author.

2. The hymn must be appropriate to the part of the liturgy in which it is sung. There is a difference here between the Anglican tradition where the hymn is essentially an accompaniment to the liturgy (perhaps a commentary upon it or an adornment of it) and the conventional Free Church pattern in which it is seen as integral to the liturgy itself. But in both cases the context of the hymn must have something to do with its choice; it must not be unrelated to what has preceded it or to what will follow it. It must not be stuck in because it is somebody's birthday or the octave of St Bartholomew. 'Praise to the Lord' which is essentially an *invitation* to

worship must not be put in at the end just in order to ensure that everybody has a good 'sing' before going out. 3. A hymn must be associated in some way with what is chosen as the main theme of the day. Again, this does not mean that the theme must be painstakingly spelt out several times so that everybody gets bored with hearing about it. There is, once more, a place for the subtle and allusive. But there must be a connection between what people are asked to *think* about and what they are asked to *sing* about. The second can help us remember the first – as Wesley realized so well. When Philip Doddridge could not find a hymn to follow his sermon, he wrote one. Our repertoire is less open-ended and may be quite small; but there remains the need for careful selection even of the little that we may have.

4. But people learn their religion not only from the words they sing but from the tunes they sing. This means that the music of Christian hymnody should be of good quality. This is an area in which opinions will clash and susceptibilities be offended. But is it not possible that flabby and trite tunes will produce a flabby and trite idea of Christianity? Towards the end of a life in which he had become acknowledged as the greatest authority on hymns in the English-speaking world, Erik Routley wrote:

> I do not believe that souls will be won for Christ by the use of texts and music that call for no discipline, that imply attitudes to which asceticism is a stranger, and that communicate everything they have to say at the very first impact. [8]

Songs

It is not easy to understand the distinction between *hymns* and *songs* that the writer to the Ephesians made; probably it was not hard and fast, and it has not been so since.

85

Nevertheless there is a kind of congregational singing that can usefully now be described as *songs*. The song is freer in its text and music than the hymn. It may be used evangelistically; the famous Sankey collection was called *Sacred Songs and Solos* and the Salvation Army continues to speak of songs rather than hymns. A quite different example of songs may be found in those of Sydney Carter; his songs are intended to make a point or to make people think. 'Lord of the Dance' has found its way into many hymn books, and is popular in schools, but it belongs very much to the uneven border-line between hymns and songs. Perhaps the same thing could be said of the charismatic choruses which have become so prolific in recent years. They are by no means always unsuitable in formal liturgy, but are often designed for the smaller gathering and the less structured act of worship.

Much of this material is ephemeral, but is none the worse for that. It serves a purpose that is useful, and sometimes very important. The easy, catchy tune can be of help at certain stages in our Christian pilgrimage. Nor does this necessarily contradict what has been written earlier about standards of words and music; the word 'pilgrimage' implies that we are meant to move – and to grow in our offering of praise as in everything else. What matters is that a congregation should offer the best of which it is capable; and that in such offering, it should be alert, attentive and enthusiastic.

The tone-deaf

This chapter seems to contain bad news for the tone-deaf. Indeed, unmusical worshippers often feel a despised or ignored minority – like those at school who do not like any kind of sport.

But singing bears witness to the truth that the whole body is meant to be used in worship. In recent years we have heard often the just complaint that our worship is too cerebral – that it gives too little opportunity for the involvement of the whole person. In the West, the normal physical expression of worship has been through singing. But it is not the only way in which that expression may be made. Liturgical dance is still very limited in use; but it can express the truths of the Bible as effectively as words or song. 'The Peace' evokes strong reactions of approval or disapproval, but it is a way of *expressing* reconciliation. There is certainly room for exploration into different ways in which there can be some bodily expression of worship; in that quest we must not forget English reserve, nor be entirely intimidated by it.

Finally, it must be remembered that participation in worship is not restricted to what we do, say or sing. Participation can be by ear and eye. Those who value the cathedral style of worship realize this. A few years ago, Dr Erik Routley suggested that some of the more intense Wesley hymns might be treated in the same way as the Psalms are treated in Cathedral Evensong.[9] To read and to listen with attention would also go some way to fulfilling Paul's longing that we might 'offer our very selves' to God.

Notes

1. Michael Perry, *The Paradox of Worship*, SPCK, 1977, ch.1.
2. Rowland Prothero, *The Psalms in Human Life*, Murray, 1913.
3. *Psalm Praise*, CPAS, 1973.
4. C. S. Lewis, *Reflections on the Psalms*, Fontana, 1967.
5. The text of Isaac Watts' Preface – is not easy to find, although it is often quoted. It was printed in early, but not later editions of his *Psalms*.
6. Wesley's Preface to the 1780 collection was printed in the 1933 Methodist Hymn Book.
7. *More Hymns for Today*, 181.

8. Quoted in Alan Dunstan, *The Hymn Explosion*, RSCM, 1981.
9. Epworth Review, Vol. 8 No. 1 contains this interesting lecture under the title 'Charles Wesley and his vigorous future'.

8. THE GOD WHO SENDS US OUT

The last chapter ended with a reference to a text. Here it is in full:

> I implore you by God's mercy to offer your very selves to him: a living sacrifice, dedicated and fit for his acceptance, the worship offered by mind and heart. (Romans 12.1)

The generation reared on the Authorized Version of the Bible was accustomed to hear that last phrase rendered as 'your reasonable service'. Now although we speak of acts of worship as 'services' we realize that we are using the word in a specialized sense. When we see the word 'services' on the motorway, we know that it does not mean Matins or Evensong, but something which one group of people offers to the rest of us. In a religious context, we probably think of *worship* as something that we do in the church building and *service* as something we do outside. We realize that worship is not meant to stop when we have gone outside the church, and that there are various forms of service to be offered within it. But still there seems to be a separation between the two activities. Yet the same Greek word has, for a number of reasons, been translated as worship and service, and this very fact points to a connection between the two.

The service of God

There are of course altogether weightier and more convincing reasons for the connection. In the last chapter, we saw how the praise of God is meant to direct the heart and mind, the will and attention to him. But there have been times, both in the history of Israel and that of the Christian Church, when the act of worship has got separated from all that should go with it, where it has become a mechanical process, where it has been a matter of form. It was against this that the great Hebrew prophets inveighed. We noted earlier that some Old Testament scholars have seen such prophets as totally opposed to the whole system of cult and sacrifice, whilst others have seen them as calling for a radical reformation from within it. No stronger condemnation can be found than that in the first chapter of Isaiah (1.13):

> No more shall you trample my courts.
> The offer of your gifts is useless,
> The reek of sacrifice is abhorrent to me,
> New moons and sabbaths and assemblies,
> Sacred seasons and ceremonies, I cannot endure.

And from the very end of the book – by a different author and at a different date and in different circumstances – comes the passage in which true fasting is seen as undoing injustice, sharing bread with the hungry and setting people free (Isaiah 58).

We have more than a few reflections of all this in the recorded teaching of Jesus – especially with regard to the Sabbath, to fasting and other outward forms of religious observance. The fragmentary references that we have to the actual forms of worship in the early Christian community show that the point of it was in danger of being missed. At Corinth the occasion became an opportunity for ostentation either by the rich (1 Cor. 11.17–22) or by those who considered themselves spiritually elite (1 Cor.14). Problems like these are endemic in the Christian community and keep reappearing in different forms. In the fourth century, Chrysostom wrote in terms which echo both Paul and the Hebrew prophets:

We must learn to be discerning Christians and to honour Christ in the way in which he wants to be honoured. I am not saying that you should not give golden altar vesels and so on, but I am insisting that nothing can take the place of almsgiving. What is the use of loading Christ's table with gold cups while he himself is starving? What use is it to adorn the altar with cloth of gold hangings and deny Christ a coat for his back? . . . Adorn the house of God if you will, but do not forget your brother in distress. He is a temple of infinitely greater value. [1]

Christian worship should always be making these things apparent to the worshippers. Christian worship is not unspecified and generalized adoration. Michael Marshall writes:

Jesus redeems our worship from being just a pleasant aesthetic indulgence by reminding us from start to finish that it was only by his incarnation that the doors of Heaven could be open to flesh and blood at all. [2]

Worship and mission

Several writers in recent years have tried to show the inescapable connection between worship and mission, and this was done in detail nearly twenty years ago in a book of that title by J. G. Davies. Professor Davies there wrote:

So worship and mission are not to be conceived as two distinct activities, the one theocentric and the other anthropocentric; both are aspects of a single divine activity in which we, through Christ, are included. [3]

Christian worship and Christian mission are inseparable. We will try to demonstrate this by looking back to the contents of previous chapters.

Two consecutive chapters were concerned with the use of the Bible and the place of preaching. Among many possible definitions of the latter, we used a simple one which described preaching as 'a means whereby the words of the Bible become the word of God for us'. Of course the word of God can be heard without benefit of preaching, yet the function of the sermon is to help us understand how the words of Scripture speak to us now. As we listen both to the Scriptures and the sermon, we are hearing of a God whose concern is always with his world and the people in it. We may vary in the kind of authority that we ascribe to the Bible, and we may vary in our estimate of how directly it can be applied to our contemporary society, but if we allow it any authority at all, then it will be a kind of 'lively oracle'. The second letter to Timothy in fact makes a quite modest claim:

> Every inspired Scripture has its use for teaching the truth and refuting error, or for reformation of manners and discipline in right living. (2 Tim. 3.16)

And those who expect to find such within the New Testament as well as the Old are likely to find with the writer to the Hebrews that

> the word of God is alive and active . . . cutting more deeply than any two-edged sword . . . sifting the purposes and thoughts of the heart. (Heb. 4.12 – 13)

For that word of God is about the nature and purposes of God which, as we have seen, are always involved with our world. As J. G. Davies writes:

> The Bible is the record of a sending God; consequently, to read it in the course of worship is to

92

present the hearers with an account of the mission of God in the past, which becomes a summons to participate in it in the present.[4]

A further chapter was concerned with prayer. The classification chosen there was that of praise, penitence, thanksgiving and petition. The point has been made several times in this book that Christian praise or adoration is not directed towards the vaguely numinous, and the wonder into which we enter is the wonder of what God has done in Christ.

We noted that the contributor to *Getting the Liturgy Right* who suggested that if we took 'power' and 'love' as concepts of God which evoke adoration,

> we must not speak of power in a manner which is cold or impersonal, or of love in terms that make it anything less than awe-inspiring in its scope and depth.[5]

To worship such a God means involvement in the mission of such a God.

Penitence – involving confession and absolution – point even more clearly to God's purpose of reconciliation. This we can know for ourselves. But its significance is beyond the worshippers gathered in one place. As Michael Perry writes:

> we must (and we can) confess not only our own sins (as far as we are aware of them) but also the unconfessed sins of the whole unbelieving world, for the world's forgiveness.[6]

If that at first sounds unreal, it becomes less so when we remember how much we are bound up with other people in sin and guilt and blame – and when we remember that the boundary between belief and unbelief is not always as

93

clearly defined as we would like to think. In the same way, the absolution or receiving of God's forgiveness flows beyond the congregation who receive it, and when, as in one form of the ASB Eucharist, this is followed by the 'Peace' then that word and gesture commit us to share in God's purpose of reconciliation and peace. For the 'Peace' does not mean, 'How do you do?' or 'Nice to see you', nor is it just a benevolent wish on the part of those who exchange it. It is God's peace that we pass on – from one pardoned sinner to another, and so to a world in need of that pardon.

Similar considerations apply to thanksgiving and petition. All prayer indeed is a means whereby we engage in mission. When we pray for the fulfilment of God's righteous and loving purposes in the world, in the Church or among those who suffer, we are identifying ourselves with that purpose. Sometimes, when we are spiritually sensitive or receptive, we can see that praying for something means that we can do something about it. Prayer for sick people may remind us that there is a sick person whom we could visit or help. Prayer for the hungry may mean that we are more generous over the Oxfam tin or the Christian Aid envelope. Obviously, prayer should result in that kind of action, and its sincerity may be questioned if we neglect that which we might do. Yet true Christian prayer is *in itself* part of Christian mission. There are things that we cannot do much about; we *are* doing something by sympathetic and imaginative prayer. This is the calling of those sometimes technically described as 'the religious'; but it is no less the calling of others – not least the elderly and housebound who may contribute very considerably to the mission of the Church by their ministry of prayer.

We have looked at some length at the connection between prayer and mission. We can consider sacramental worship more briefly. In the sacraments, the purposes of God are disclosed in actions – through the pouring of water, or the taking, blessing, breaking and distributing of bread and wine. In both Baptism and Holy Communion, God's redeeming purposes are made clear to us not only by what we say but by what we do. Over the bread and wine we recall above all a God who has sent his Son. The breaking of the bread, although in itself a practical preparation for eating, never ceases to remind discerning Christians of Christ's body broken for them; in receiving the elements they receive the body and blood given for them, and, when the action is complete, respond by saying together 'Send us out . . . in the power of your Spirit . . .'. William Temple, war-time Archbishop of Canterbury, used to say that the greatest moment in the Communion Service was when the worshippers went out to serve God faithfully in the fellowship of his Church.

A faulty connection

If worship and mission really are two sides of a coin, why is the fact not more evident? Why should it be necessary in the final chapter of this book to explore a connection that surely should not need explanation or even declaration?

We know that the connection has not been obvious throughout Christian history, and that it is not obvious today. For this, there are all sorts of reasons. The first is that worship can become too formalized in the sense that the form can take over as some sort of end in itself. After great services in a cathedral, those who have some responsibility for them sometimes say to one another, 'it went very well'. All sorts of things may be implied by that – the choir didn't break down in the middle of a psalm, the canon-in-residence did not forget his reading-glasses when he went to the lectern, and the Bishop did not accidentally take the prayers from the Burial Service when he was conducting a wedding. This book has stressed time and again the importance of careful preparation for worship, and the need for attention to detail. But there remains the danger that in doing these things we leave others undone, and that we become absorbed with the success of the forms and orders that we have striven to perfect. We need to hear Charles Wesley's warning:

> Oft did I with the assembly join
> And near thine altar drew:
> A form of Godliness was mine,
> The power I never knew. [7]

Secondly, worship can become too individualized. We can suppose that it all exists for the benefit of ourselves. 'I didn't get much out of it', is generally condemnatory of what has happened. The words, 'I like', become the final arbiter in matters of worship – if 'I like' it, I'll join in, and if I don't, I'll opt out. Many years ago, before lay administration of the chalice was common in the Church of England, a layman of unquestionable godliness was authorized to help at Christmas, and a member of the congregation was afterwards heard to say, 'That spoilt my communion'. The phrase 'my communion' has been pushed out by all the pressures of the Parish Communion movement, but the same attitude prevails. So long as people think of worship as organized for their private spiritual titivation, there will be little sense of it as an embodiment of the mission of God. Sometimes the trouble arises because people think of public worship as an extension of private prayer, but the reverse is nearer the truth. At Baptism, we were received into the Christian society, and our personal prayers are therefore an extension of the prayers of the Church.

Finally, we must notice again that which was underlined in the first chapter. The primary in worship is so often obscured by the secondary. This has been a recurring feature in the history of Christian worship; reformations of one kind or another try to set it right, but it is not long before the process starts again. This has been illustrated earlier, and further examples need not be quoted. Liturgy does not have to be stripped of all that adorns it; but at intervals we ought to ask whether the adornments have not become more important than the liturgy itself. This is never an easy question to raise because it touches on the work (and sometimes the vested interests) of some very devoted people – choirs, servers, flower arrangers and the like. Not long ago the writer preached at a Harvest Thanksgiving where bread and grapes were piled so high upon the altar that the cross was almost invisible. This could be a parable of our worship and its priorities.

Restoring the connection

The last twenty-five years have seen a quickening of conscience about the connection between worship and service in the world. One way in which this has been expressed is in special services which have emphasized the connection. Thus in the country, there has been some revival of Rogation and Plough Sundays to supplement and perhaps in some way to correct the ever-popular Harvest Thanksgiving. Industrial festivals have had some popularity in urban areas, and at least they go to show that God is Lord not only of the natural order, but of a technological society. The desire from a variety of organizations – from the Red Cross to the British Legion – for what in Scotland is sometimes known as 'kirking' arises from a variety of motives; but the occasions have within them the potential for demonstrating the essential connection between worship and service.

Apart from one very important respect which we shall

consider at the end of this chapter, the chief contribution of mainstream liturgical revision to the reunification of worship and service has been in the flexibility which characterizes most contemporary acts of worship. An example of this may be found in the arrangements for intercession in the Anglican Eucharist. The Prayer Book form was significantly introduced by the words 'Let us pray for the whole state of Christ's Church militant here on earth' and the prayer that followed was an accurate picture of Tudor society. Government is by the sovereign and Privy Council, and ministers of religion consist of bishops and curates. No reference was made to education, hospitals or world peace. It was customary for many years to preface the prayer with a series of biddings which might supply some of the matters omitted. But since Series 2 (1967), it has been legitimate and usual to bring all sorts of concerns within the prayer itself. The Rite A introduction is 'Let us pray for the Church and for the *world* and let us thank God for his goodness', and, as we have seen, the intercession need not even include a set form of words. Similarly in the ASB Marriage Service permission is given to include prayers which have been chosen or composed by the couple in consultation with the priest. What actually happens as a result of this may be quite stereotyped; but built into it is the opportunity to think afresh about the life we lead, the world we inhabit, and the will of God for both.

But alongside official revisions there is the unofficial work of those who have written and collected prayers for use in existing services. Such men as Frank Colquhoun in the Church of England and Caryl Micklem in the Free Churches have been responsible for books that rouse the Christian conscience to contemporary needs in intercession, as well as the prayers themselves which reflect those needs. But out society is so fast-moving, that as soon as any anthology is published, gaps within it become apparent.

Another contribution has come with hymn-writing. As the last chapter showed, one manifestation of the 'hymn explosion' is the number of texts concerned with the social outreach of the Gospel. The collection *100 Hymns for Today* strongly emphasizes this concern. It includes Fred Kaan's *Magnificat Now* which begins:

> Sing we a song of high revolt;
> make great the Lord, his name exalt:
> sing we the song that Mary sang
> of God at war with human wrong.   (No. 86)

A famous Dean of St Paul's in the earlier part of this century, W. R. Inge, had said that the Magnificat was more revolutionary than 'The Red Flag' but few people had actually believed that about it or seen it as a song of 'God at war with human wrong'. The hymn quoted has been severely criticized on stylistic grounds; it is not the best effort of a distinguished contemporary hymn-writer, and probably will not long survive. But it has made people think; it may have inspired others to write better verses, and the approach it took at least caused the editors of the collection to seek out other material, to realize that men like Wesley and Doddridge were not lacking in a social conscience, and to include items from their writings not previously well known. The same general thrust, in a rather different form may be found in the selection of hymns both in this collection and in its successor which are designed for use after communion and which are often variations of the theme, 'Send us out in the power of your Spirit'.

Ending worship

The second chapter of this book closed with a practical section concerned with immediate preparation for worship; this chapter will close by giving particular attention to the way in which worship should end.

Revisers of the Eucharist have been at one in their insistence that the act of the communion is the climax of the service and that what follows should be very brief. Series 2 had a prayer which became very popular and included the words 'Send us out into the world in the power of the Spirit'. The prayer lost the phrase 'into the world' in later revision; and everyone closely associated with the structures of church life knows that there is plenty of 'the world' within them, and that we do not go out of a wholly perfect society into one that is wholly evil. Rite A has an optional sentence, optional hymn, choice of post-communion prayers, optional blessing and mandatory dismissal. The Roman Catholic Mass has prayer, simple blessing and dismissal, the Methodist rite a very short mandatory prayer and dismissal with hymn and blessing optional, and the United Reformed order of worship a similar conclusion with a prayer which begins with thanksgiving that God has fed and renewed his people and then goes on:

> Now we give ourselves to you
> and we ask
> that our daily living
> may be part of the life of your kingdom,
> and that our love
> may be your love reaching out into the life of the world. [8]

There is thus considerable unity of thought in the way these services end. A hymn is clearly optional; as we have seen, some fine hymns have been written for this point in the liturgy, and there are other great hymns (e.g. 'Forth in thy name') which could scarcely be sung at any other point. If a hymn is used, great attention must be paid to its character; it must have something to do with our being 'sent out', and if a general hymn of praise is chosen in order to give everybody a 'good sing' it merely brings the service back to where it started, and ignores what the conclusion of it is meant to be. It thus becomes one of those adornments which, as we have seen, so easily obscure rather than illuminate the liturgy. The blessing is optional in some of the rites quoted; many believe that it is superfluous since there can be no blessing greater than the one which has been given in the communion itself. What is mandatory in all the rites quoted above is the *dismissal* 'Go in peace to love and serve the Lord' or words to that effect. It is imperative that such words should be the *last* spoken in the act of worship, and their significance is totally missed if anything else follows.

Two practical objections are sometimes made here. The first is that a hymn is necessary 'to get the choir out' to which the answer is that most of them are capable of walking on their own feet without vocal accompaniment. It would be symbolic if the congregation followed the choir and clergy from the church, and this gives rise to another objection that people need a time of quiet reflection before leaving. But so do the choir and clergy; and a period of corporate and complete silence between the communion and the dismissal could most effectively meet this need.

The word 'Mass' is thought to derive from the traditional dismissal formula *'Ite missa est'*. Although hallowed by use, it is hardly descriptive of what has happened in the act of worship. But rightly understood, it can make clear the connection with which we have been concerned – that the God who calls us to himself is the God who sends us out to share in his eternal purpose of reconciliation. For service in the world is the inescapable consequence of true Christian worship.

Notes
1. St John Chrysostom, *Homily 50*, 3 – 4.

2. Michael Marshall, *Renewal in Worship*, Marshall, Morgan & Scott, 1982, p.143.
3. J. G. Davies, *Worship and Mission*, SCM, 1966, p.71.
4. Davies, op. cit., p.130.
5. See chapter 5 note 9.
6. Michael Perry, *The Paradox of Worship*, SPCK, 1977, p.82.
7. *Wesley's Hymns*, 91. (88 in original 1780 collection)
8. Book of Services, St Andrew Press, 1980, p.40.